I
Might
Just Be Right

*For Coral Siby,
with thanks for taking
care of my chiclets*

[signature]

I
Might
Just Be Right

JOHN MARTIN MEEK

To order additional copies of this book, contact:
Xlibris Corporation
1-888-795-4274
www.Xlibris.com
Orders@Xlibris.com
26887

If you have a dollar bill and I have a dollar bill and we exchange them, then we each end up with a dollar bill.

But if you have an idea and I have an idea and we exchange them, then we each end up with two ideas.

Thermo Tungsten, Philosopher

Contents

Acknowledgements

When I decided to do this collection it seemed getting a manuscript together would be a piece of cake. After all, most of the writing already had been done. However, it turned into a major effort.

I want to thank Lew Ferguson, a friend from our days as journalism students at the University of Oklahoma, a retired bureau chief for the Associated Press and as of this writing a member of the Kansas Board of Regents for Higher Education. I asked Lew for his advice and counsel on several matters relating to the book's content. He understands that when I ask his advice I want it hard and to the point, and he is very accommodating.

Finally, I acknowledge with gratitude Jim Kiser's willingness to write the foreword. When he emailed it to me, I sent this email back to him: "Your words are both flattering and undeserved, but I am immodest enough to use them anyway."

Preface

There was an old Scot in the Washington, DC area who was a well-known atheist. But at a cocktail party one evening he mentioned to a friend who knew him well that he had been in church the previous Sunday.

His friend was surprised the Scot had been in church, a place for believers in God. He said, "Sandy, everyone knows you are an avowed atheist. What the hell were you doing in church with all those believers?

"B-e-e-e-cause," stuttered the old Scot, "god-d-d-d-ammit, they m-m-m-might just be right!"

Newspaper columns obviously are opinions of the writer whether it is as a sportswriter in a small community or by nationally syndicated sparklies such as Maureen Dowd, George Will and Ariana Huffington. As it is with human nature, all columnists wish you to remember those where their opinions turned out to be right, and forget the ones where they were nowhere near hitting the mark.

Growing up in Western Oklahoma in a very small town called Rocky, my major hero was Ernie Pyle, the Scripps-Howard columnist and war correspondent killed in the Pacific in World War II.

My mother and I eagerly awaited every Pyle column. One of my older brothers spent much of the war in the Pacific with a Navy dive-bomber squadron. We didn't expect Ernie to write about him, but identified very much with the other servicemen who were the subjects of Pyle columns.

Selecting journalism as my major after I finished five years active duty with the military, I wanted to be the next Ernie Pyle. My first opportunity came during my last semester at the University of Oklahoma when I was selected to be editor of The Oklahoma Daily, OU's student newspaper, in the fall of 1955.

I wrote editorials for the paper, and an occasional column called "Meekly Speaking."

Later, after earning an MA in journalism at Syracuse University, I was offered the very coveted position of television editor and the column that went with it at the Syracuse Post-Standard. It was a nine to five job, five days a week in an era when accepting junkets to New York City and Hollywood was routine for television editors/columnists.

I turned it down because I simply did not care about who was doing what in television. And while I'm grateful to the Post-Standard editors who had so much confidence in me, I never have regretted the decision.

Upon retirement from a career in communications, mostly in Washington, DC, I moved to the Tucson area and for two years taught journalism courses at Pima Community College. During this time I kick-started my old journalism career. Among the writing I did was an occasional guest column for the Arizona Daily Star.

My first column submissions, and not a one was used, were to the sports department discussing the stupidity of comedian Dennis Miller being hired as part of ABC's "Monday Night Football" broadcast team. Though none of my anti-Dennis columns were printed, it was one of those situations where I can at least say I was proved to be right.

For columns or other material I have written in recent years, I stuck to the same criterion I had used oh so many years ago while editor of The Oklahoma Daily. I have tried to write only on subjects where I had some knowledge.

I have had a fantastic career, doing things I could never have dreamed about growing up in Rocky. Fate did not deem that I become the next Ernie Pyle, and in my opinion neither has anyone else. And, I *might* just be right.

John Martin Meek

Foreword

To me, the opinion writer has the most challenging—and the most rewarding—job of all journalists.

To high school students assigned to write about their opinions, it initially seems such an easy assignment: All they have to do is let those squiggly feelings flow out onto the paper.

Similarly, many email writers have adopted that same attitude—as I noticed frequently when my job required me to read all the letters submitted to the newspaper editor for publication.

But the reality is that good opinion writing is difficult, sometimes painfully difficult.

The opinion writer must get his or her facts straight, as a good reporter must. Then the opinion writer must go two significant steps further. He must fit the facts into a framework and make the relations between the facts clear. And then, he must tell the reader what this all means.

To me, it is exciting to write a good commentary. And it is almost as exciting to read a good commentary. Indeed, I have come to prefer to gather my facts from a well-researched and documented commentary than from news stories.

This is all a way of saying that in publishing this book of commentaries and features, John Martin Meek has taken on a tough job. Fortunately, he can do it.

I know Meek in three ways: as a journalism teacher, whose class at Pima Community College I spoke to; as a writer of Guest Opinions to the Arizona Daily Star while I was editorial page editor; and as an email correspondent the past several years.

He is a man of strong opinions and keen insights, and he has the ability to state them forcefully yet gracefully.

As you read through this collection, you will find his feature on Olympic Gold Medal winner Terry McCann having to outwrestle his own self-doubts is compelling and inspirational.

I loved the Mozart story with which Meek ends his commentary titled, "Let's hear it for the loners." I won't tell it here so you will have the pleasure of seeing it in context.

Then there is Meek's painful and insightful commentary on the death of a young serviceman, titled, "Ex-Marine Shares Sense of Duty Felt by Fallen Heroes."

Being in the military was important to Meek, as was his early desire to write about it, a desire honed by his reading of Ernie Pyle in World War II.

However, as Meek says in his introduction, "Fate did not deem that I become the next Ernie Pyle."

Well, nobody else became the next Ernie Pyle, either. But Meek shares one important trait with Pyle: He tells good stories.

To me, that is the highest praise a writer can receive.

**—Jim Kiser, former editor of the editorial page,
Arizona Daily Star, Tucson, and now
an award-winning columnist for the paper.**

Political

Don't Worry Democrats.
Help Is on the Way

Several days ago USA Today devoted an entire page to what many believe is the Democratic Party's sordid plight. The illustration on the page depicted a donkey eating from a feedbag strongly resembling an elephant's trunk.

Bill Clinton gurus James Carville and Paul Begala gave their views in a two-column litany of George W. Bush's horrendous mistakes from the economy to his badly botching of our foreign policy. And they offered suggestions for change.

In newspaper jargon there also was a "box" listing the Democrats' "shifting message" (actually messages) since Nov. 2.

Recently in my local Tuesday morning coffee group a political veteran said the Democratic National Committee was helpless to effect change. Apparently he does not remember a football-shaped Ohio Republican Chairman named Ray Bliss who came out of nowhere to resurrect the GOP after Barry Goldwater's disastrous 1964 campaign.

Now former Vermont governor and presidential candidate Howard Dean is chair of the Democratic National Committee.

From his new bully pulpit, perhaps the man who taught us how to raise millions on the Internet can out Ray Bliss Ray Bliss.

He has the energy, the smarts and the experience to do just that. Terry McAuliffe, his predecessor put in place by President Clinton, was a virtual political unknown but he knew how to keep the DNC's checks from bouncing.

Once in presidential politics candidates waited to near the election year to announce. We can give George McGovern, after running a pathetically frivolous campaign for the Democratic nomination in 1968, credit for early starts. Hardly had Richard Nixon taken the oath on Jan. 20, 1969, when McGovern said he would seek the nomination in 1972. Unfortunately, he got it and created a world-class fiasco for the Democratic Party.

But, Democrats, do not fear. Help is coming.

It will be in the person of U.S. Sen. Hillary Clinton (D-NY). And as of today there is no Democrat visible who can stop her juggernaut once it starts rolling.

The Clintons are smart. Just remember how in 1992 a young governor from the little state of Arkansas known but for his womanizing, unseated a man who probably was the most qualified person ever to be president.

And when the entire right-wing movement with millions to spend had four years to shut him off from a second term, Bill Clinton triumphed again.

If you had access to Hillary's complete body of work since she came to the Senate four years ago, Democrats and Republicans might be aghast to learn she has teamed up on legislative matters with virtually every GOP member who tried to impeach or otherwise discredit her husband's presidency.

Revenge for Monica and Jennifer? Not at all. It's called political strategy and when the time comes you will see the brilliance of her work. And, as First Lady, she may not have corralled the massive health care industry in her ill-fated attempt, but that she tried will earn her respect among millions of Americans with no health care at all.

And what Republican can beat her?

Rudy Giuliani? In 2008 his extraordinary presence as mayor of New York during 9/11 will be as long forgotten as President George H.W. Bush's stunning victory in Operation Desert Storm.

John McCain? He is a man of great respect nationwide for his Vietnam War heroism and stand on numerous major issues. But does he really have the fire in the belly for another race for the GOP candidacy?

Jeb Bush, Santorum, Frist and Brownback? Not even on the radar screen.

We can't predict what issue Hillary will have with the economy in 2008 but at the rate gas prices are rising, American, Delta, United and U.S. Air will be bankrupt unless bailed out by Uncle Sugar. With those carriers grounded, most commerce will stop as it did after 9/11.

And the Iraq War? It may be the issue. Both WMD commissions have reported in now and it is a slam-dunk—not one clue of any kind.

What was John Kerry thinking, a Vietnam veteran of all people, when he said in the last campaign he would have our troops home by the end of his four-year term. At least he was partially right. Those who are killed or wounded will be back and the numbers grow daily.

My God! Fifty-four years ago I was fighting a war in Korea. Today, there are still 34,000 American troops there—almost a third of our U.S. Force in Iraq. And on Tuesday Gen. Richard Myers, chair of our Joint Chiefs of Staff, is quoted in the Star as saying after two years the Iraqi insurgency remains "undiminished." It's going away by 2008?

Whatever the issues, when the 2008 campaign gets underway the Republicans will need some new attack dogs in Congress. Because Hillary will only have to remind the old ones that they were in bed with her on issue after issue.

So trust me, Democrats, help is on the way.

Postscript: This column was submitted to the Arizona Daily Star in April, 2005, but not used, largely because Tucson is the base of the Democratic Party in Arizona. In the past it produced the noted Udall brothers—Stew and Mo. Both served in Congress. Stew spent eight years as Secretary of the Interior under JFK and LBJ and still is active in the environmental movement. Mo, one of the best storytellers in the history of the Congress, once made a run at the presidency. Example of Mo's humor: When Jimmy Carter was president, some brewery came out with a Billy Beer named for the president's brother. At a media dinner, Mo said in his remarks that someone had sent a can of Billy Beer off to a lab to be analyzed. The lab report that came back said, "Sir, your horse has diabetes."

'Getting Some of His Own' No Help for the Bush Girls

No one, most especially those who dislike the father and his policies, should take any joy from the alcohol-related problems of First Daughters Barbara and Jenna Bush.

The reason is that while the Bush Administration continues the practice of pouring billions of dollars down the anti-drug rat-hole, our nation will go on ignoring the enormous toll alcohol wreaks on the powerful and powerless alike.

And Grandmother Barbara Bush contributed nothing of a positive nature by saying in a recent speech that her son the president was "getting some of his own."

What Mrs. Bush does not seem to realize is that President Bush already has "enough of his own" without the embarrassment brought about by twin teenage daughters being caught violating Texas liquor laws.

In the presidential campaign last year, the media spared no time or expense in its collective search for evidence George W. Bush had used hard drugs. They apparently failed.

In time, however, it was established that Mr. Bush's drug of choice had been one perfectly legal and socially acceptable. It was alcohol, and the news of a DUI arrest and other bits of information carried by the media indicate our president is a recovering alcoholic.

In Washington, no doubt some media members threw back a couple of shooters at cocktail hour and congratulated themselves on having vetted Mr. Bush on cocaine or other hard drug use. No one bothered digging into a most appropriate question: how was Mr. Bush handing his alcoholism?

Most drug abuse experts will tell you that with true alcoholics, the first and last thought every day is the need to have a drink.

And while there are many exceptions, most recovering alcoholics need the tried and proven support system provided by Alcoholics Anonymous.

Does Mr. Bush attend AA? If so, where? What message might he have for other alcoholics that would offer them hope in dealing with this life-long ordeal? What counsel can he give Barbara and Jenna, his daughters?

Having personally worked numerous public events with the Secret Service, I promise there is no way a member of the First Family can go to a bar, restaurant or nightclub without every single employee of that establishment knowing about it.

For Barbara and Jenna to so blatantly flaunt the law in their efforts to be drinking with their peers may be a gross lack of common sense, but their actions also may well be cries for help.

If they already are alcoholics at their young ages, they need professional counseling. If they are just trying to embarrass their father they have succeeded in a spectacular manner, and it's time the parents took them to the figurative woodshed.

Why do I care?

A few weeks ago before teaching my first class of the day at Pima Community College in Tucson, I opened an email message to learn a young woman who once worked for me had died. She was the third and last of three women, all world-class drinkers, who were on my staff at the same time. One was a former White House aide and together they were three of the smartest, most talented people of many who have worked for me during my career.

If I had known then what I now know about alcoholism, I sincerely believe there is a fair chance all three might still be alive today. That I did not have that knowledge when I might have helped them is something I will regret forever.

Postscript: This column was written, as most of my columns have been, for the Arizona Daily Star in Tucson. For a reason I can't recall it was never submitted to the paper.

After having gone though the well-known drinking problems of her son, President George W. Bush, I was amazed at the apparent ignorance of Barbara Bush about alcoholism and the flip way she handled it in her public comments.

It seems to me it would have gained President Bush a great deal of political capital had he asked his mother to head up a national educational effort about alcoholism, as well as being more open about how he came to the decision to get sober and stay that way.

Waving Goodbye to President Kennedy

I t is an image that will stay with me forever.

President Kennedy was leaving the White House for the last time, as he walked to the helicopter on the South Lawn to begin his Texas trip on Nov. 21, 1963.

He left the Oval Office on an overcast and misty morning, giving a warm smile and a jaunty wave at the four of us standing just a few feet away.

I waved back.

Our group included the late journalist, Sarah McClendon; Ben Blackstock, Oklahoma Press Assn., and Barbara Gamariekian, White House press office.

At times like this at the White House, minds usually do not wander into the horrors such as what might happen the next day when Lee Harvey Oswald assassinated our president.

Most historical narratives agree the president was going to Texas on a Democratic Party diplomatic mission to resolve a major conflict between Vice President Lyndon B. Johnson, Gov. John Connally and Ralph Yarborough, Texas' senior senator in Washington.

I have never bought this scenario.

What I believe was happening was the former Democratic Senate Majority Secretary, Bobby Baker, LBJ's boy in very way except genetic, had become a great embarrassment to his "father." Baker's alleged handling of campaign donations and other unethical and/or unlawful acts was one of the biggest scandals in Capitol Hill history.

Bobby Kennedy had done his best to get LBJ dumped after JFK named the Texan as his running mate at in 1960. Now, Bobby had the scandal as ample ammunition to convince his brother there should be someone new in 1964.

Back home in Texas, which was what mattered most to LBJ, these rumors were devastating to his large but tender ego. I believe LBJ persuaded JFK to make the Texas trip to quash those embarrassing whispers.

With JFK, LBJ and Sen. Yarborough all in Washington, DC, it begs the question: Why not just invite Gov. Connally to come there instead of laying on a two-day presidential visit to the Lone Star state?

At the time, many of JFK's major legislative goals were languishing in Congress. Sen. Bob Kerr (D-OK) was no longer there to work magic for his leader.

For whatever the real reason the trip was made, up to the point of the gunfire in Dealey Plaza it was a triumph in every way.

At the White House on Nov. 21, after the Marine One helicopter was airborne with the president and Mrs. Kennedy, Sarah left our group. Barbara, Ben and I went into the Oval Office.

Barbara opened a drawer in the president's desk and pulled out candid photos of little John-John and Caroline playing around their father's office. These photos, when released, became some of the most poignant images ever from the White House.

With the president now gone I wanted to try out his famous rocking chair, and thus became the last person to sit in it.

Atop the president's desk, was a coconut shell. On it was scrawled the message leading to his crew's rescue after PT 109 was sunk in the Pacific during World War II.

The last person to meet with President Kennedy on Nov. 21 was Admiral Tazewell Shepard, his Naval aide. Years later Admiral Shepherd was an usher at a Washington, DC church where I was a member.

I always wanted to ask him what this last meeting with the president was all about. But, I never did. And why, after 40 years, does it really matter.

On Nov. 21, 1963, I was press secretary to the late U.S. Sen. J. Howard Edmondson (D-OK).

Postscript: This feature was used in the Daily Oklahoman, Oklahoma City and The Oklahoma Daily at OU on Nov. 21, 2003, the day before the 40th anniversary of President Kennedy's assassination.

An Oath . . .

Soon after moving to Arizona in the fall of 1999, I decided to ease into retirement teaching a journalism course at Pima Community College, Tucson, and jump-starting my journalism career.

One outlet for my writing was a political "webzine" called Gridlock Mag, which had been created a few years earlier by my youngest son, James, several years before he made the transition from cyberspace to real world journalism.

Unfortunately, after years being the only political webzine based in Washington, DC, with contributions mainly from White House correspondents and other journalists, Gridlock at this time is on hold somewhere in cyberspace and not available any longer on the Internet.

The next year, 2000, created a bonanza of opportunities for Gridlock pieces with the presidential campaign, two national political conventions and cabinet confirmations for Dubya Bush—to say nothing of the Florida voting fiasco.

Be warned, readers, modesty has no place in this book. Apparently I was the first one to dub Sen. Lieberman, Al Bore's running mate on the Democratic ticket, as "Holly Joe." It was picked up and used by several publications including The New York Times. (Sorry, Senator, it has nothing to do with your being an Orthodox Jew. It's about your acting holy.)

After the election the confirmation hearings for former U.S. Sen. John Ashcroft (R-MO) to be President Bush's first attorney general were rancorous from the beginning, even though he was trying to be approved by his own Senate colleagues.

Ashcroft was neither popular during his time in the Senate nor a star in the Republican Party galaxy. His primary fame seemed to be as a member of a musical group with other members of the Senate. And his "holier than thou" fundamentalist Christian beliefs were considered by many as over the edge.

What inspired this column was an effort led by Arizona's Republican junior senator, John Kyle, to convince Senate members that, if confirmed, Ashcroft would abide by his oath and not carry his questionable beliefs to the job as this country's chief law enforcement official.

Obviously he was confirmed. Whether he abided by his oath as one of the most controversial Bush cabinet members the first four years is to view his record and make your own decision.

An Oath Is an Oath Is an Oath

Some of Sen. John Ashcroft's supporters and defenders, such as Sen. John Kyle (R-AZ), have been on national television saying that when President Bush's nominee for U.S. attorney general takes the oath, he will be true to those few words that have to be uttered by most officials serving in our federal government

Sen. Ashcroft, of course, will take the oath and put a special verbal explanation point at the end with his "So help me God!"

Surely by now we recognize the oath for president of the United States, attorney general or private in the Marine Corps is worth exactly what FDR's Vice President, John Nance Garner, said was the value of his own office—a warm bucket of spit.

Proof. You want proof?

Let's start with the highest office in the land.

Did taking the oath deter Richard Nixon and his gang from trying to cover up the illegal acts of the Watergate scandal, including the cover-up of the cover-up?

Did it stop Ollie North from playing God with our laws and our democratic system in the Iran-Contra scandal?

Did the oath stop Bill Clinton from bringing great personal disgrace on the office of the presidency by having kinky sex with a young woman just a little older than his daughter in various White House locations?

Did a similar oath make any difference to Ricky Ames of the Central Intelligence Agency when he fed the Russians secrets leading to our spies being killed so he could indulge his fantasies of living like a millionaire?

Nope.

This is not to suggest in any way that Sen. Ashcroft, as attorney general, might engage in the kind of criminal conduct of corrupt politicians or spies.

The point is an oath really is just so many words.

How many politicians, public servants, members of the military and law enforcement officers say to themselves before their wrongdoing, "Oh, gee, should I be doing this? I think it might violate my oath of office."

Hee hee.

An attorney general has so much flexibility in enforcing the laws of the land that he can do what he damned well pleases and still live with his or her conscience in carrying out the oath of the office.

What part of the oath guided Janet Reno, the Clinton AG, in making what amounted to an Iwo Jima-like assault on the Branch Dravidians at Waco?

She could not have known it would in time lead a mad man to blow up the Murrah Federal Building in Oklahoma City, the boldest act of terrorism in the nation's history (prior to 9/11).

Or on a more positive note, what part of the oath led attorneys general under Eisenhower and Kennedy to order U.S. Marshals to integrate high schools and universities in the south?

In nominating Sen. Ashcroft, President Bush hardly could have chosen a more divisive person to head the U.S. Department of Justice—a hypocritical act for a man constantly mouthing platitudes about uniting our country. But, then, when he made the nomination he had not yet taken the oath as president.

Oaths are totally worthless. And in falling back on this buttress, Ashcroft defenders picked a bed of quicksand on which to defend the attorney general nominee.

Those who take oaths could not repeat the words five minutes later to save their lives. But more important, many do not remember the *intent* of their oaths

Postscript: After Attorney General Ashcroft pushed through the Patriot Act and presided over the depriving of due process for the prisoners held at the U.S. base in Guantanamo, what more need be said about his four years in this powerful office?

No Washington Spin

Who would have thought it? Public relations, one of the most maligned professions in America, now is being called upon to save our nation.

Among some thinkers, a good PR program for our country may be more important than B-52 bombers, special operations forces and aircraft carriers. This notion gained a great deal of cachet recently when Russian President Vladimir Putin told Barbara Walters of ABC-TV that the U.S. was losing the PR war against terrorism and Osama bin Laden.

Putin's candid views have been punctuated by caustic columns critical of the Bush Administration's failure to rally foreign allies to our cause and cartoons such as one that ran Oct. 29 in the Arizona Star. It showed a man with a briefcase confronting three clowns lounging around a Ringling Brothers Circus travel trunk.

"Oh, I'm sorry," said the man. "I mistook you for the government's bioterrorism response planners."

"Hey," said one of the clowns, "It's a natural mistake."

Exactly how did our government get to where it desperately needs PR help in the war on terrorism? Like this:

It all began on 9-11 when the White House gave an implausible explanation why President Bush, leaving Florida, headed for a military bunker in Omaha instead of returning to Washington.

The next misstep was when Vice President Cheney went on TV a few days later and strongly implied he was running the country on 9-11while President Bush in Air Force One was still circling Moose Jaw, Montana.

Almost immediately, President Bush nailed Osama bin Laden as the evil force behind the 9-11 events. Would it really spoil one of life's vast eternal plans if we were given just a clue or two as to how he so quickly came to this conclusion?

Then, when anthrax arrived, HHS Secretary Tommy Thompson, using 50-year-old data, did a media blitz assuring Americans it was no real problem.

Having spent much of my career in political and private sector public relations, allow me to offer a few gratuitous suggestions to the federal government on how to improve its PR effort in this strange war.

1. **No spin, please.** Crisis PR is not about smoke and mirrors or "spin." It is about taking a negative situation, making the necessary changes for improvement, then telling the world about these changes. It's really that simple.

2. **And no spinmeister.** We do not need a federal communications czar as some have suggested. For decades the White House has had communications directors (e.g., David Gergen who did it both for Reagan and Clinton) who orchestrated all federal entities so they spoke with one voice. If the person who now has this job can't do it, presumably Gergen again would be available.

3. **Ignorance is no sin.** The great humorist Will Rogers once said, "We're all ignorant—just on different subjects." It's still okay to tell the truth including admitting ignorance. Too many feds tried to be PR experts on anthrax when in truth they knew almost nothing, and the resulting flow of information was disastrous.

4. **Make a plan.** The biggest vacuum in 99 percent of all PR operations is the lack of anything resembling a crisis plan. All Washington entities should be making one. Unfortunately, chances are they will have an opportunity to use the plans in the future and hopefully will get it right the next time.

5. **Define "them."** Muslims outnumber us 1 billion to 300 million, not good odds in any war. Our government should spend whatever time it takes assuring the Muslim world that our war is against the terrorists, not against a religion. This message must be repeated over and over again here and abroad.

6. **Keep it impersonal.** In the waning months of his presidency, President Johnson talked to White House visitors in terms of the Vietnam War being between him personally against Ho Chi Minh. President Bush needs to quit building up bin Laden as "the" enemy and make it the war against all terrorists.

7. **Don't sell more eggs than your hens can lay.** Shortly after 9-11, Secretary of State Powell promised the world immediate proof that bin Laden was the culprit. While Powell may have spoken from sure knowledge, the world is still waiting and the secretary has discovered that even old hands can learn new lessons in this new kind of war where this great general has no battle scars and no medals.

Postscript: This column ran in the Star on Nov. 29, 2001, as our federal government was still somewhat at sea in deciding how we could be viewed more positively by the Muslim world. As this is written in May, 2005, Muslims around the world are rioting over what apparently was an erroneous Newsweek article about the Koran being desecrated by U.S. interrogators.

If We Lose Doris and Michael, We May Lose all Our History

M y fellow cyberfolk, please join me in this fervent prayer: "Heavenly Father, we come to you today to pray for the health and hopefully long lives of Doris Kearns Goodwin and Michael Beschloss. May you be with them always as they share their knowledge and wisdom of history with those of us in their various television audiences. Amen."

The 2000 Democratic National Convention has just ended and, according to my stopwatch, Doris and Michael managed far more minutes on prime time television than Al Gore, the anointed candidate. Back in the Gore War Room in Nashville, Gore's strategists must be wondering how two boomer historians could possibly upstage their candidate at a four-day convention they, along with the Clinton White House, controlled minute by minute.

We wonder, too. When we see Doris and Michael holding forth all across the television spectrum as the only experts on history and the presidency, it brings to mind a rhetorical question once posed in The Washington Post about the venerable Bob Straus, a Democratic National Committee Chairman. Over the years in the Washington media Straus became known as "Mr. Democrat."

"Who," someone asked rhetorically on the Post editorial page, "elected Bob Strauss as 'Mr. Democrat?'" And we ask, plaintively, who designated Doris and Michael as the only two historians in America? Roone Arledge at ABC? Les Crystal, Jim Lehrer's producer?

Whatever happened to the history department at Harvard? Where is Arthur Scheslinger Jr.? So he's a little long in the tooth. So is Andy Rooney, who's old enough to be Arthur's father. Where are all those other scholars of the presidency, the authors of books about Reagan, Carter, Ford, Nixon, Kennedy, Eisenhower, Truman, et al? Has history been abandoned on the campuses of Yale, Princeton, Georgetown, and Cornell?

Fellow cyberfolk, this is a real crisis. Just think. If anything were to happen to either Doris and Michael, who are not spring chickens, television news would not be able to tell us who was president before Bill Clinton, the name of President Reagan's wife, and exactly who was that former president who blasted a Washington newspaper music critic who dared pan his daughter's singing ability?

Picture this. Cokie and Sam are on their ABC program one Sunday morning talking presidential politics. Doris and Michael are absent. Sam turns to Cokie.

"International events can hurt a president running for reelection," says Sam. "Remember during the Iran hostage crisis when President . . . President . . . I'm sorry, Cokie, but who was the president running for reelection then?"

"Oh, my, Sam," says Cokie, "For the life of me I cannot remember his name. He was from the south, as I recall. Had a big southern accent." Turning to George Will, she continues. "George, you have a wonderful memory. Who was that president?"

"I'm sorry," says George, "I know it wasn't Homer or Plato, but beyond that . . ."

"Well," says Sam, "if Doris and Michael were here we would know. Anyway, as I recall the Iran hostage crisis did hurt this guy and I think he was defeated."

"Yes," says Cokie. "That president definitely was defeated. It's just a shot in the dark here, but as I remember the man who defeated him was George Bush."

This is a hypothetical situation, of course, but not beyond reality. If this really happened then millions of Americans would go to bed not only puzzled, but perhaps even thinking George Bush and not Ronald Reagan succeeded Jimmy Carter. It would be terrible, with no other historians in America to set the record straight.

And a final point. We have no idea what America's only historians are paid for their television appearances. Since Doris and Michael seem to be the only historians, that would indicate their fees might be fairly high.

Assuming this is so, we would think Doris might take a hint from Barbara Wa Wa, Regis, Kathie Lee and Frank, Bill Plante of CBS and countless other television personalities and spend a few bucks for, at a minimum, an eye tuck. As for Michael, I thought we would never live to see any man whose hairpiece could be worse than the dead squirrels worn by Charlton Heston and the late Howard Cosell. But we have.

Postscript: This is one of three articles/columns I wrote for the Gridlock Mag webzine during or immediately after the 2000 Democratic National Convention in Los Angeles.

I'm Running for President
Now You Take My Family. *Please!*
Were Democratic Convention Television Viewers more Gored than Bored?

Bob Novak, newspaper columnist and CNN talk show tongue-wagger, was a guest on Larry King's show immediately after the Democratic National Convention of 2000 faded with the sunset over the Pacific Ocean. According to Novak, the Los Angeles convention was the worst in history.

Clinton, Novak said, ruined the four-day event with his ego trip speech on Monday night and it was all downhill from there. Gore's speech was a total failure.

Earlier on Jim Lehrer's PBS news show, Mark Shields, newspaper columnist and regular contributor, trashed the convention's little staged panels which did come off like high school plays. Someone remarked about the irony of a convention held in a city with a million show biz producers whose services were not used to turn out slick convention productions, as opposed to the amateur panels.

It is the nature of Democratic national conventions to be circuses. Their history is rich with smoke-filled rooms, deals with bosses, and stories such as the one about Bobby Kennedy trying to force LBJ to take himself off the ticket after JFK had named him as his running mate.

Los Angeles likely will be remembered as the "family" convention.

On Monday night, Hillary became the first sitting First Lady to address a Democratic National convention. With frequent television "pool" shots of her daughter, Chelsea, on the stage, she also introduced her husband, the president of the United States and titular head of the Democratic Party, for his farewell address.

From then on for the next four days it was a blur of Gores and Liebermans. It wasn't that many of them were so awful, like Jimmy Carter's family, but that there were so awful many of them. The grand finale was the Gore daughter introducing her mother who introduced her husband for his acceptance speech.

Who was the great political genius to be credited for dreaming up this family scenario? And where was James Carville when Al Gore needed him?

Traditionally, these introductions before live television audiences were assigned to men and women who held some political coin spent on the candidate in the past or would be in the future. It was always assumed the candidate's family was 100 percent on board, and didn't need to be given major political favors at the convention to assure continuing loyalty.

While the polls today showing George W. Bush with a comfortable lead over Al Gore probably mean little with months to go before election day, the Gore campaign can benefit from all the political stroking possible on a convention program.

For example, where was Mayor Rich Daley of Chicago? Or the prominent also-rans in the vice presidential selection process, such as Sen. John Kerry of Massachusetts? And especially missing were prominent military figures such as Admiral William Crowe, the former Joint Chiefs chairman, who backed Bill Clinton.

Traditionally, too, in modern history the Democratic candidates were careful to pay homage to the party's leaders in Congress. The presidential campaign once was a team event with the congressional races. But Jimmy Carter's relations with congressional leaders were so strained that when his chief lobbyist paid a first visit to House Speaker Tip O'Neill, he was told to leave and never come back. Bill Clinton did not meet with Democratic congressional leaders from the end of the 1992 Democratic convention in New York until the Sunday after his election, when they came to dinner at the governor's mansion in Little Rock.

There is always the question of how family really plays in a presidential campaign or even after the election. While Gore's daughters were beating the drums for daddy, Al Jr. was making national headlines by getting a speeding ticket in North Carolina. In fairly recently times, LBJ, Nixon, Carter, Reagan and Clinton have had their embarrassments with close relatives while in the White House. A few days after Carter was defeated by Reagan, a New York television talk show host quipped, "Carter would have been better off had he been born an orphan."

Probably Los Angeles will be the pinnacle of the candidates' families dominating a convention. Those who were there or watched the convention on television can decide on their own if they were either Gored or bored or both. But, to paraphrase Comedian Henny Youngman, at the 2004 Democratic National Convention the candidate should have been saying, "Now, you take my family. *Please!*"

Postscript: This is the second piece written for Gridlock Mag relating to the 2000 Democratic National Convention.

Picking a Second Fiddle
To Play While Rome Burns

Polls say most Americans don't care who is No. 2 on either ticket. Remember Harry Truman, LBJ and Jerry Ford? Spiro Agnew and Dan Quayle? Think again.

TUCSON, AZ (Special to Gridlock Mag)—It is nothing short of ironic that one of the best Dan Quayle stories to come out of the George Herbert Walker Bush presidency involved Dick Cheney, then secretary of defense. It went like this.

When Eduard Shevardnadze became the Russian foreign minister, President Bush sent Jim Baker, his secretary of state, to Moscow to check out the new guy. When Baker and Shevardnadze met, the foreign minister thought he would take Baker's measure with a riddle. The foreign minister told Baker that one day he was watching a parade with a friend and the man turned to him and said, "I understand the father of the man leading the parade is a friend of mine, but I don't know who the father is."

Shevardnardze replied, "Brothers and sisters I have none, but that man's father is my father's son." The foreign minister then asked Baker if he could figure out who was the father. Baker, no fool, said, "The father was you, Shevardnadze."

When Baker came back to Washington and reported to President Bush, he told him about Shevardnadze's little riddle. Bush liked the story and the next time he saw his vice president, he repeated it and asked Quayle if he knew who was the father. Quayle said, "Sir, could I get back to you on this?"

Quayle returned to his office. He decided Dick Cheney was the brightest member of the Bush Administration, so he called him.

"Dick," said Quayle, "I have a little riddle for you. You are watching a parade with a friend and he says, 'I understand I know the father of the man leading the parade, but I can't figure out who he is.' So you say to your friend, 'Brothers and sisters I have none, but that man's father is my father's son.' Who is the father?"

Cheney immediately says, "The father is me, Dick Cheney."

Quayle thanks Cheney and hangs up. The next time he sees Bush, the president asks Quayle if he has solved the riddle. "Yes sir, Mr. President," says the vice president, "The answer is me, Dick Cheney."

Maybe this story literally drips with irony. Because, for one thing, among the numerous smart, capable and otherwise competent Republicans who might have been chosen by Vice President Bush as his running mate in1988 was Dick Cheney. There's more than a fair chance that had Cheney been on the ticket, the Bush Administration might have lasted eight years instead of four.

There is further irony in the media stories that former President Bush played a big role in helping Gov. George W. Bush select Cheney as his running mate. If this is true, it's hard to imagine George W. would not have turned to his father at some point and asked, 'Hey, pop, where was Dick Cheney when you were looking for a running mate?"

While to most Dick Cheney's selection was a big surprise, he wasn't exactly somewhere out on the plains of Wyoming herding cattle. Having come to Texas to head the Halliburton Company, one of the great old service businesses in the oil industry, Cheney instantly became something more than "all hat and no cattle" among the Texas business establishment and the state's Republican Party.

It's also interesting that Gov. Bush chose Cheney to do the running mate search, departing from the usual stupidity of having a Washington lawyer handle the dirty work.

Why does it always have to be a Washington lawyer who puts together the list? Why does the chicken always cross to the other side of the road?

It's clearly a political myth that Washington lawyers know more than anyone when it comes to such matters. Their keen legal minds, most presidential candidates believe, can sniff out skeletons rattling back there in the closets and other possible pitfalls each potential veep might have to mar the ticket. Washington lawyers are all considered wise beyond their years, even though some—to paraphrase George Wallace—can't even park their Mercedes straight. If you are a presidential candidate, it normally is simply mandatory that you hand over the veep vetting to a superlawyer such as Warren Christopher, Lloyd Cutler, Vernon Jordan or John Reilly.

John Reilly? Well, maybe it's better not to have your John Reilly. It was John who did the Mondale running mate search in 1980 and brought forth, ta da, Geraldine Ferraro. At least John did not fall so far from Washington guru disgrace as the person who convinced George McGovern that Tom Eagleton was the perfect running mate. It fits in with Gary Hart's many political blunders that he was the searcher, or at least the one with the second to last approval.

What Vice President Gore wouldn't have given to be able to sit down with JFK, LBJ and even his late father to get some advice on this subject before he made the bold move of naming Holy Joe Lieberman.

He knows he could have asked President Clinton, but wouldn't have gotten a straight answer. He could have asked

Jimmy Carter, but who would want the advice of the man who picked Walter Mondale as his running mate? He could have asked Walter Mondale, but bringing up memories of Geraldine Ferraro might have been a very sore subject. He could have asked McGovern, but, like the rest of the world, George wouldn't be able to remember the other name on that ill-fated ticket. (It was, first, U.S. Sen. Tom Eagleton of Missouri, later dumped, then Sargent Shriver.)

But Gore did not vary from the Washington lawyer routine. Following Clinton's example, he put this heavy burden on the slender, pinstriped shoulders of former Secretary of State Warren Christopher of O'Melveny & Myers.

An excellent choice. Warren Christopher, though not a sparkling secretary of state (Is it any secretary's fault that he/she has to follow Henry Kissinger?), is a class act. Before Clinton leaves office, he should bestow upon Christopher the Medal of Freedom with a dozen Oak Leaf clusters for his untiring work to free the hostages held by Iran; getting Congress to lift the arms embargo against Turkey, our NATO ally; heading up the Clinton-Gore transition team, and countless other services to his country.

From Richard L. Berke's article in the July 9 New York Times Sunday Magazine, we knew many of the people Christopher considered and the questions he asked these leading Democrats. Also from Mr. Berke, we know Gore's single criterion, (repeated at the first Gore/Liebermanfest on Aug. 8) for the person he wanted to be Gore's Gore: someone capable of taking over the job of president at a moment's notice.

With all due respect to Mr. Christopher and the vice president, these distinguished gentlemen need a reality check.

Before either Bush or Gore made their choices we saw the lists for both candidates and there were no obvious losers. After all, if some small-time county commissioner, machine politician from Missouri can by default become one of the greatest presidents in our history, should we have been concerned about House Minority Leader Dick Gebhardt or dropout GOP presidential candidate Liddy Dole?

Here, Mr. Gore and Mr. Bush, are the real questions you should have been asking all your potential running mates:

Are you an alcoholic? Alcoholism is an epidemic in this country and among politicians is pandemic. Why? Putting aside the pressures of public life, drinking is to politicians what honey is to bees. Voters would be shocked to learn how many of this country's leaders were or are world-class drunks. The media reports on all sorts of national political hanky-panky but rarely, except for the long ago Wilbur Mills incident, gets into the problems of alcoholism. But historians never have been reluctant to tell and retell Sir Winston Churchill's fondness for the spirits.

Are you gay? A "yes" answer to this question would not help any ticket.

Do you believe in God? Any person occupying the Oval Office needs to believe in a higher power just to keep things in perspective. By contrast, presumably some of our major adversaries such as Adolph Hitler, Joseph Stalin and Saddam Hussein did or do not. We know both candidates would never ever close a major speech without the obligatory, "And, God bless America." But, what do these men and their running mates really believe?

Do you have a heart? While many tough decisions await every president, such as sending our armed forces into harm's way, most of the day-to-day decisions by a president have to do with the common welfare of all Americans.

It has been written that JFK never saw real poverty until he campaigned in West Virginia in 1960. Having a heart to understand the plight of those deprived of equal justice and opportunity may transcend all other qualifications for this high office

In the end, let's be brutally honest. Having two people on the ticket is something we just do.

Every now and then we do lose a president in office. In my lifetime that sad event has given us Harry Truman, Lyndon B. Johnson and Jerry Ford. They held the nation together in difficult times and achieved more good than anyone would ever have guessed when each became vice president. And we can be very thankful to have missed Spiro Agnew and Dan Quayle.

Absent the untimely passing of the president, all vice presidents spend four or eight years playing second fiddle while Rome burns. Asked recently what he had done as vice president, Gore responded that he had stood by his president.

That he has done, standing with eyes cast to the sky and whistling softly while the impeachment roll call on Clinton droned on in the Senate chamber. Just as Hubert Humphrey kept justifying Vietnam for LBJ and Gov. Bush's father saw no evil, spoke no evil and heard no evil during the Reagan ordeal over the Iran-Contra scandal.

Why, on the wild chance that Ross Perot might have won in 1992, does anyone seriously think we would ever have seen Admiral Stockdale again for the next four years? And, would anyone besides Mrs. Stockdale have cared?

Postscript: The first two articles on the 2000 Democratic National Convention were written somewhat with tongue-in-cheek. But every time I think of Dick Cheney being president of the United States, I want to pray for the protection and good health of George Bush.

Once There Was a Man from Oklahoma Who Ruled the World

By John Martin Meek

WASHINGTON, DC.— Looking back from the perspective of the 40th anniversary of the 87th Congress in January 1961, you can forget most of those sayings attributed to the late U.S. Sen. Robert S. Kerr, possibly the most powerful member of Congress in the last century. Especially you can forget this one, "I'm against any combine I ain't in on."

Now dead for 38 years, Kerr in that Congress used his great power to pass three major bills into law that had no direct effect on his Oklahoma "combine," but would serve his country well for decades.

In 1961 everything was changing. John F. Kennedy had been elected president and Kerr's seniority, hard work and some unusual circumstances positioned him with enormous, almost unprecedented, influence in the 87th Congress.

No one has since come close to holding the kind of power he had on Capitol Hill. It's likely no one ever will. From '61-62 he personally crafted three bills that would change America and, to some extent the world, forever.

The three bills: 1) authorization for NASA to begin a project to send U.S. astronauts to the moon, 2) the Trade Expansion Act of 1962, and 3) the Communications Satellite Act.

"If this Congress had passed no measure other than the Trade Expansion Act of 1962," Senate Majority Leader Mike Mansfield said at the end of the session, "it may well have won a role among the most significant Congresses of American history."

Shoot the Moon

With Lyndon Johnson's election as vice president in 1960, Kerr moved into this important Senate space committee chairmanship controlling NASA.

Kerr also was ranking, or second highest Democrat, on the Senate Finance Committee. On the Senate Public Works Committee, Kerr already had all the pork barrel projects under his thumb as chair of the Rivers and Harbors Subcommittee. Here, too, Kerr became de facto chair of the committee because Sen. Dennis Chavez (D-NM), the actual chair, was seriously ill and had no energy for dealing with Kennedy's vigorous New Frontier.

One of the first major bills for Kerr in that session was the National Air and Space Administration's Apollo Program.

In a hastily called Joint Session of Congress on May 25, 1961, Kennedy surprised the nation with these words: ". . . I believe that this nation should commit itself to achieving the goal, before this decade is out, of landing a man on the moon and returning him safely to the earth."

Where Kerr was concerned, what JFK wanted, JFK usually got. A bill asking for $5.4 billion to fund the moon project was introduced and in short time President Kennedy signed it into law.

Behind the scenes, Kerr also used his considerable influence to see that the Senate Appropriations Committee approved the funds.

Most Americans felt it patriotic to support the NASA programs and compete with the Soviets.

But the trade bill that came before the Senate Finance Committee was another matter. When trade legislation gets serious attention in Congress, all friends and foes come out from under their rocks.

While Kerr could see how a trade bill would in some ways work well with his favorite Oklahoma project—to make the Arkansas River navigable from Tulsa to the Mississippi—it really was not about Oklahoma. It was about the country and its place in world trade for the future.

"There is no doubt the Trade Expansion Act of 1962 was one of the most important laws in history," said Robert Novak, the syndicated columnist and television commentator. (Novak at the time reported on the Senate Finance Committee and other Senate business for the Wall Street Journal.)

The 'Uncrowned King' of the Senate

Kerr's third major achievement of the 87th Congress also was his last, as he dictated the structure of the organization created to handle peaceful space telecommunications in the Communications Satellite Act.

There, Kerr, who wanted a mostly private-sector corporation, found himself out front in a ferocious battle with Senate liberals such as Paul Douglas (D-ILL), who wanted a government entity to do the job.

It was partly in anger, partly in frustration, partly out of admiration that Sen. Douglas stood on the Senate floor one afternoon and labeled Kerr as "the uncrowned king of the Senate."

Kerr had the votes and, in the end, the Act created the Communications Satellite Corp. (ComSat), a private company.

"It's difficult to overstate the influence of this legislation in the perspective of 38 years since it became law," said Henry Goldberg of Goldberg Godles Wiener & Wright, a Washington, DC, telecommunications law firm.

"It was the first public dividend of the U.S. space program," said Goldberg. "Not only did it revolutionize communications in this country, it is not too much of a stretch to say that it played a significant role in the demise of the Soviet bloc."

Goldberg said ComSat's funding helped Western Union launch Westar I, which Ted Turner used to create his superstation and CNN through cable TV and revitalized a stagnant cable industry.

"ComSat in 1964 gave birth to Intelsat which now has 144 member nations involved in satellite programs," said Goldberg, "and the law's influence even affects the dot.com world we live in today."

Lessons in Power

After the 1962 elections, Kerr's cover had been blown. He was no longer just the "pork barrel king" of Oklahoma.

The national media had been given a good lesson in power by Kerr during the last two years and they were waiting. Among publications planning cover stories on Kerr for January, 1963, were Time, Life and The Saturday Evening Post.

About this time, Kerr had his first heart attack. Then, on the morning of Jan. 1, 1963, as the Oklahoma Sooners prepared to play Alabama in the Orange Bowl, he suffered another heart attack and died at age 66.

Instead of major cover stories heralding Kerr's status as the powerful new statesman in Washington, there were obits hardly mentioning the legislation he pushed through the 87th Congress.

Oklahoma got everything Kerr asked for those last two years including a personal visit by President Kennedy to spend the night at the senator's ranch near Poteau. The U.S. Corps of Engineers agreed to hasten the completion of the Arkansas River Navigation Project by several years and some of the NASA largess began to trickle into Oklahoma industries.

"We knew he always took good care of Oklahoma," said Novak. "But for the last two years of his life, he also took good care of his country."

Postscript: I served as press secretary to Sen. Kerr during the 87th Congress. This feature was used in the Tulsa World as an entire page, with a large photo of Kerr with the U.S. Capitol in the background, on Sunday, Jan. 7, 2001. To the best of my knowledge, this is the first time Kerr's unprecedented service to his nation in this Congress has been told in detail in books or otherwise.

Sports

University of Arizona Athletic Officials Can Learn A Lot from Oklahoma

Statistically there is not much to compare between the University of Arizona and University of Oklahoma football programs.

The Wildcats have no wins and one tie (with UCLA) for a conference championship, and have never played in the Rose Bowl. Their bowl game record generally has been dismal.

Oklahoma has won several national championships, numerous conference titles and enough major bowl trophies, if melted down, to build heroic-size statues of former OU coaches Bud Wilkinson and Barry Switzer.

Now both schools have shared the shame and embarrassment of having had several members of their football team making news by allegedly breaking the law.

True, the charges against the Sooner players were far more serious than the recent allegations against the Wildcats. At OU it began when one player shot another in the exclusive athletic dorm. Next, also in the dorm, several players allegedly gang-raped a young woman. Then the starting quarterback was caught in an FBI sting selling cocaine. He achieved the ultimate in disgrace for his university by appearing on the cover of Sports Illustrated in his orange jail jumpsuit.

Just prior to these alleged crimes, the NCAA placed Oklahoma football on probation. What a wonderful situation inherited by an acting university president, David Swank, OU's law school dean, who wanted the job on a permanent basis.

While the football players faced criminal charges, all fingers were pointed at Coach Barry Switzer. As the crisis reached almost daily national media attention, my firm was asked to provide pro bono public relations services to help OU dig out of the mess.

We had all-day meetings with Swank, Switzer, Athletic Director Donnie Duncan and the university's own PR team. My business partner, Jim Hartz, the former "Today Show" host, held practice "meet the media" sessions for Switzer and Swank. Then I stayed several days in Oklahoma preparing a long-range plan centered on making changes in the football program to prevent future incidents, not trying to put a positive spin on the alleged crimes.

During this time I talked to numerous people in the university community about the root causes of a great football program gone awry. Everybody had the same answer: Barry Switzer was just too lenient with his players.

Shortly afterward, Switzer lost his job and Swank went back to the law school.

The message here for University of Arizona officials, and not just the athletic department, is that if you have a bunch of bad apples you best send them packing before Arizona becomes another Oklahoma.

Coach John Mackovic in his second season is under great pressure to produce a winning team and fill those empty seats at the Arizona stadium. But with the Cats ranked near the bottom of the PAC 10 in preseason polls, would dumping a few players really matter?

If anyone thinks such action would be the end of the world for Arizona, then take a look at the post-criminal Oklahoma football program.

Yes, with Switzer's departure there was a dark period for OU fans with three less than glorious seasons and no television as part of the NCAA probation. Once coveted seats for Sooner games in OU's Memorial Stadium became plentiful.

The people of Oklahoma, who for 40 years used winning Sooner teams to prop up the state's self esteem, discovered their real sense of worth in the aftermath of the Murrah Building bombing and a devastating tornado that ripped through Oklahoma City and other communities.

After leaving OU Barry Switzer became the Dallas Cowboys coach and led them to victory in Super Bowl XXX. Recently he finally was elected to the College Football Hall of Fame. Duncan later left to be a senior executive for the Big 12 Conference.

Two years ago the Sooners under Coach Bob Stoops returned to college football big time by beating Florida State 12-3 in the Orange Bowl, and being crowned the 2000 national champions.

Getting rid of Wildcat players who may think they are above the law will send a message to all future Arizona athletes that this type of behavior will not be tolerated. If this means a losing season or two, as happened at Oklahoma, then for the school and the state it is well worth the wait.

Postscript: This column ran in the Arizona Daily Star on Aug. 16, 2002. The Arizona Wildcats ended their season that year at 4-7. The punishment given the players who were in trouble was to spend a day helping build a house in the Habitat for Humanity project. According to news reports, the players quit working and left as soon as the TV cameras were gone. Coach Mackovic was fired before the end of his third season, and in time was replaced by Mike Stoops, who had been working with his brother Bob, coach of the Oklahoma Sooners. Everybody together now, let's sing the chorus. "It's a small world after all."

'Big Red' and Oklahoma

(Originally published in December, 1955 in The Oklahoma Daily, the University of Oklahoma campus newspaer.)

To carve anything substantially great out of land that was long ago described as a desert was certainly a tremendous challenge as well as a task for those early-day pioneers who settled in Oklahoma Territory in the late 1800's.

But down through the years those pioneers and the generations who followed have fought to overcome obstacles that have faced Oklahomans since our state was a bare prairie. They have battled drought, floods, pestilence, and depression and wear the scars of all those mighty conflicts.

And they have faced the shame of carrying a gunnysack to the county seat for "government relief" and that spread by writers who never really knew or understood the problems of our people.

They have searched many times for something to cling to in those years which would give them the pride to hold their heads high, but even in the time of prosperity they often have failed to find it.

Although those pioneers may have been shortsighted in some of their planning for the future generations, they had foresight in realizing the need for a state school and in 1892 founded the University of Oklahoma.

Soon after the university came into being, a limited sports program was organized and since that time has had a gradual but steady growth. Like the state, the school also has had its ups and downs.

The university's football team, under Bennie Owen and his successors had its place as the foundation was laid for better things to come. These "things" did come too with the debut of Bud Wilkinson and a fine array of assistant coaches and outstanding players.

Mr. Wilkinson proceeded in the very short time to build here a football team that has gained worldwide recognition and this year, for the second time, was named national champion.

OU has seen good teams before but there was something different about the Wilkinson product. It ceased to be the team for the university or the students or the alumni. It became the team for all of Oklahoma and for all Oklahomans. From the Panhandle to the Kiamichis, from Grand Lake to the Red River it became the "champion" for all our people.

It became a team for the old and young alike. Whether they knew the difference between a field goal and a punt mattered not, it was their team and it won consistently. Whether they were a sand hills farmer or a Tulsa oil millionaire mattered not, it was a team for everybody.

If we ever had any doubts of this, they were completely wiped out recently as we walked down the streets of Norman. Two aged farmers clad in overalls and blue denim shirts stood talking and as we passed by this conversation was overheard:

"My brother-in-law was up here from Texas for Thanksgiving and we were talking a little bit about football so's I said to him, 'You reckon you got airy team down there that can beat OU?'"

Now that the OU team is the established "champion" for the state, it has heaped new responsibilities on the shoulders of the coaches and players. They will be called on again and again as they have been in the past to muster that "something" that turns defeat into victory. They're no longer playing for the school alone—they are playing for the state.

They have given Oklahomans their Alamo, their "Marine Hymn," their Empire State Building, and their Pike's Peak—and it is their duty to always maintain the highest standards for sportsmanship with the keenest desire to win.

Then it is very appropriate that the team be called the "Big Red." For "Big Red" is the spark that has ignited the greatest fire of state pride the State of Oklahoma has ever known.

Postscript: I know I'm reaching for it when I include an editorial written when I was editor of The Oklahoma Daily at the University of Oklahoma. It appeared on Dec. 7, 1955, in a special edition of the Daily honoring the Sooners for their second national football championship. It is only my opinion, but I think what I wrote 50 years ago has stood the test of time.

One Olympic Gold Medal, Many Miracles:

The Untold Story of How Tulsan Terry McCann Outwrestled An 'Unbeatable' Russian and His Own Self-doubts.

By John Martin Meek

DANA POINT, CA (Special to The Tulsa World)—It was the summer of 1960. He was a small young man, dressed in a warm-up suit, standing in the predawn darkness on a bridge over the Tiber River running through Rome. As he leaned over the rail and looked into the dark waters below, he saw in his mirrored reflection a face full of guilt and self-doubt.

Hours earlier, after being defeated in an Olympic wrestling match with an unheralded Finn, Terry McCann had walked away from his wife, the U.S. Olympic team wrestling coach and his teammates. Demoralized by this early defeat in his quest for Olympic gold, McCann had decided he would not return the next day to face Michail Shakhov, a Russian considered unbeatable in the freestyle event. All through the night hours he aimlessly wandered alone (he thought) through the streets of Rome.

The match scheduled for the next day with the wily Russian was just the latest of many obstacles McCann had faced on the road to Rome, all of which he had somehow miraculously overcome. Working as production manager for the U.S. Junior Chamber of Commerce national headquarters on Boulder Park in Tulsa, McCann had injured a knee and was awaiting surgery just as the U.S. wrestling trials for the 1960 Olympics were being held.

McCann was heartbroken but helpless. But, a U.S. Olympic Committee under pressure to make a decent showing in 1960 against the awesome Soviet athletes, came to his rescue with the first "miracle." For the first time in history, the USOC made an exception for McCann and let him move on to tryouts for the American team. They were being held at the University of Oklahoma under its wrestling coach, Port Robertson, who had been named coach for the U.S. Olympic wrestlers.

McCann drove to Norman from Tulsa and beat three opponents. Then, another disaster struck. He was hospitalized and in a coma due to dehydration. When he regained consciousness, Coach Robertson was there to tell him that under Olympic rules he must wrestle Dave Auble, a three-time national champion in the 125.5-pound weight class, the very next day.

The news stunned McCann. He told Robertson he could not possibly compete again without at least three days of rest. Discharged from the hospital and deeply depressed, he drove back to Tulsa.

"It was miserably hot," says Robertson. "We had no air-conditioning in the dorms and the athletes couldn't sleep. The wrestling rooms were even worse. And Terry was not the only one who quit and went home."

Terry's wife, Lu, had made as many sacrifices as her husband in his quest for Olympic gold. She had worked four years in a factory in Chicago, where they both were reared, to help put him through the University of Iowa. There, McCann had won national championships and been an All-American three of his four years.

But at Iowa McCann's overwhelming dislike for losing also caused him to quit school three times and go back to Chicago, once after a practice loss to a teammate.

Lu McCann tried to persuade her husband to go back to Norman for the final match, but with no success. As a last desperate effort, she called Ben Swanson, executive vice president of the national Jaycees and McCann's boss.

Swanson immediately summoned the production manager to his office and, in a typically blunt manner, gave McCann an ultimatum. Either go back to Norman and wrestle Dave Auble or go somewhere else to work.

"I wasn't afraid of Dave Auble or anyone else," says McCann. "I was so weak I thought I would lose, and I just couldn't face it."

But, McCann got in his car and drove straight to Norman where the second "miracle" happened. Still tired and wrestling in the sweltering rooms under OU's Owen Stadium in 105-degree heat, McCann defeated Auble and earned his coveted trip to Rome as a member of the U.S. Olympic team.

But in Rome, McCann's major opponent continued to be his own self-doubts—and with good reason.

"The year before a U.S. wrestling team met the best of the Russian wrestlers for 100 matches both here and in the Soviet Union," McCann recalls. "In 100 matches, we won seven and had one tie and all the wins and the tie were mine.

"The tie was with Shakhov. But under Olympic rules, I had to pin him to win. The Russians had never, ever been pinned. And with five points against me after losing to the Finn, a loss to Shakhov and another point would have finished me in Rome."

McCann also attributes his demoralization and the loss to the Finn to a freaky screwup by Olympic officials.

The morning of this preliminary match, all events were canceled due to rain. Later in the day, they were rescheduled but no one bothered to wake up McCann before the U.S. team bus left for the wrestling venue. When he awoke, he grabbed his gear and took a taxi to the match. But, not being with the team, security officials would not admit him. When he finally talked his way inside, there was no time for a warm-up.

"Terry had a bit of a temper," says Robertson. "No athlete ever trained harder and no one hated to lose more than Terry. He was very competitive. But I never knew until today that he did not plan to wrestle Shakhov."

As McCann stood in deep despair on the bridge near dawn, he felt someone put an arm around his shoulders. It was Doug Blubaugh, another wrestler who had been so concerned over McCann's walking out on the team that he had followed him in the shadows throughout the night.

In that moment with his teammate he faced the crux of his young life. Despite his deep hatred for losing, he knew in his heart he could not disappoint his wife, Coach Robertson, his teammates and the many friends, neighbors, and others who believed he would bring home the gold.

Together, the two athletes went back to the Olympic village to get some sleep. When the time came later that day for the showdown with Shakhov, McCann was there to walk out onto the mat for the most important match of his career.

"When we got to Rome," says McCann, "the Russians already knew about my knee operation. They had me targeted as a sure loser."

But, there was yet another "miracle," and as it often happens in life fame can be quickly won or lost. Only 18 seconds after the McCann-Shakhov match began, the "unbeatable" Russian had been pinned.

Three other successful matches followed the Shakhov victory. When they were over, it was Terry McCann who stood on the highest level of the presentation stage. While "The Star Spangled Banner" was played and more than 5,000 people cheered, an official draped an Olympic gold medal around the Tulsan's neck.

After the Olympics the McCanns flew back to Tulsa, where they lived at 6738 E. 9th St. Swanson and a few friends were at the airport to meet them. The next day he went back to work at the Jaycee national headquarters.

Terry and Lu McCann established a major beachhead in Oklahoma during their 10 years in Tulsa. Five of their children were born there.

A younger brother, Jimmy McCann, came to OU on a wrestling scholarship but left to join the Marines. He was sent to Vietnam and his name is now etched on the black granite wall of the Vietnam Veterans Memorial in Washington, DC.

Another brother, Fran, wrestled at Oklahoma State and later was an assistant wrestling coach there on his way to becoming head coach at Notre Dame.

McCann, 66, now serves as executive director of Toastmasters International at its headquarters in Mission Viejo, CA. He will retire next year.

Through the years he rose in the Olympic hierarchy to serve on the board of directors and executive committee of the U.S. Olympic Committee, as head of the U.S. wrestling federation and as a vice president of the international wrestling federation.

The McCanns live comfortably a few miles from the Toastmasters' headquarters in the oceanfront community of Dana Point.

They fondly remember their days in Tulsa when Terry went off to win one of the few gold medals the U.S. Olympic team, which included Rafer Johnson and Wilma Rudolph, brought back from Rome in 1960. The other two golds won in wrestling were by Blubaugh and Shelby Wilson, former high school teammates at Ponca City.

But Terry McCann still remembers the night he outwrestled a life of self-doubt while standing in the darkness on a bridge over the Tiber River. And that victory, he says, was in the end the final "miracle" in his long journey to earn Olympic gold in Rome.

Postscript: It was just a few days from the opening of the 2000 Summer Olympics in Sydney, Australia, (Sept. 15, 2000) when I sent a query to Wayne Greene, an editor at the Tulsa World, about doing a feature on Terry.

Back then, Terry and I were on the staff at the U.S. Junior Chamber of Commerce national headquarters in Tulsa. We didn't socialize outside of work, but it is fair to say we were friends.

Approval for the feature came back from The World three days before the Olympics opened in Sydney. I hastily made airline arrangements and the next morning flew from Tucson to Los Angeles, where Terry and his wife, Lucille, picked me up at LAX.

From the airport we stopped in Torrance to buy some exotic fish for the pond in their back yard, then spent most of the day with the interview and reminiscing about the early days of our careers with the National Jaycees in Tulsa. After a dinner on the water in Dana Point, where they live, Terry and Lu drove me back to LAX for the flight to Tucson.

Back home, I spent most of the night writing the feature about Terry and emailed it to the World then, because I did not yet have a digital camera, sent the photos I had taken by FedEx.

The feature ran on the World's front page the day the Olympics opened in Australia.

It's amazing what we can forget, regardless of age. During our hours of conversation I spent with Terry and Lu at their home in Dana Point, I said looking back it now seemed incredible that we as his associates at the Jaycee headquarters had not done anything special to see him off on his trip to Rome, or to welcome him back with his gold medal.

"That's not true," Terry said. "There was a special lunch with staff members at a nearby restaurant and I was presented with a sports bag for the trip."

"You're kidding. I don't remember that."

Terry then named the restaurant, which was across the big park from the Jaycee office. He also remembered other details. "You are the one who organized the luncheon," he said, "and the person who gave me the sports bag. Do you think I would forget something like that?"

Well, I will be damned. I guess it's just another of those senior moments

It's Time for Dennis To Go

Pardon me, Dick Cheney, for borrowing a line from your vice presidential acceptance speech at the GOP convention, but it's time for him to go.

"Him" is Dennis Miller, the most miscast person on national television since Phyllis George, a former Miss America hosting a morning network show, tried to get a convicted rapist to hug the woman who had lied to put him behind bars for years.

Dennis is the "three's a crowd" commentator with Dan Fouts, former NFL quarterback, and Al Michaels on "Monday Night Football" on ABC. He was put there to work magic by Executive Producer Don Ohlmeyer, who has impressive credentials as a television magician.

Television is one of the most brutal and fickle of all businesses. It reminds one of the old saying about business success, i.e., "The higher the monkey goes up the flag pole, the more we see of its rear." Just ask Bryant Gumbel, who reigned as king on NBC's "Today Show" for years and hasn't had a decent rating day or night since.

Normally, as television heartlessness goes, Miller and Ohlmeyer both would have been history by now with a Monday night show that makes us even miss Frank Gifford. But, no. Ohlmeyer's security blanket is the legacy of Roone Arledge, who long ago took ABC's decent news organization and turned it into various versions of "Hollywood Squares."

There must be some way for Ohlmeyer and ABC to drop Dennis and save face here. They want humor? Someone who knows slant patterns and end runs? A real in-your-face commentator with whom all us guys can identify?

Could someone please email Bob Dole's phone number to ABC Sports?

Postscript: I take my NFL football seriously. Anyone who has read my novel, "The Christmas Hour," knows the Washington Redskins are mentioned from cover to cover. Incredibly, ABC Sports kept Dennis around for a second season of Monday Night NFL football. By then, I think even Dennis' mother must have been shuddering every time he opened his mouth in front of the microphone.

I also have long questioned the journalistic ethics of ABC News in terms of the programming on "Good Morning America." When I lived in DC, GMA originated its show or shows from Aspen in the winter and at least once from Alaska. There, Charles Gibson and Diane Sawyer are in bright sunshine when in fact Aspen or Alaska would be pitch black at that time of the morning. No acknowledgement that the segments were shot the day before when the sun was shining. In Arizona (three hours later in the summer time zones and two hours in the winter) occasionally ABC's "Nightline" will have "Recorded Earlier" on the screen at the opening of the program. If the program came to Arizona viewers live in its 10:30 p.m. slot here, it would be 1:30 a.m. back in DC.

On Monday, May 30, 2005, The New York Times had an article on how close GMA is coming to overtaking the top-ranked "Today Show" in the ratings game. When David Westin, president of ABC News, was asked by the Times reporter how he reconciled the use of outtakes of ABC's popular show,

"Desperate Housewives" on a program operated by the News division, the response echoed the written-in-stone approach of the late Roone Arledge.

"It's always been the case in the morning programs that there is an entertainment element," Westin said. "I have no doubt our audience is very happy to see those 'Desperate' outtakes." So there, the gospel from the president of the News Division of a national TV network that promotes itself as a major watchdog of government and private sector ethics.

Me Thinks He Protests too Much

In 1984, the Baltimore Colts football team was moved in the middle of the night to become the new franchise for Indianapolis. At the time it was suggested that since the Colts had been moved by Mayflower Van Lines, they might change their name to be the Indianapolis Pilgrims.

The Baltimore mayor immediately put together a privately funded committee to get the city a new football franchise. My firm in Washington, DC was hired to ask Congress to pressure the National Football League into creating new franchises for Baltimore, Oakland, and several other cities wanting a team.

Working with former Washington Sen. Slade Gorton, now serving on the 9/11 Commission, we were able to get a bill through the Senate Commerce Committee forcing the NFL and major league baseball to add new franchises.

At the time NFL Commissioner Paul Tagliabue was still the NFL lobbyist in Washington, and we met a few times to discuss Baltimore's situation. As they say on the street, he seemed to be a stand-up cat.

Tagliabue was confident Congress would do nothing. When the Senate Commerce committee passed a bill creating new teams, the NFL's massive lobbying machine crushed Sen. Gorton and me like so many ants under a boot.

That was then and this is now. When Tagliabue did his TV apology for the Jackson-Timberlake 2004 Super Bowl fiasco, denying the NFL knew what was going to happen at the half-time show, it was one of the greatest acts of hypocrisy in recent sports history.

I'm not a prude, but in a way Jackson's juvenile juke with Timberlake was somewhat minimized by the major part of the show.

In the regular NFL football season, TV cameras rarely use a shot showing anything below the waist of cheerleaders with such teams as the Washington Redskins and Dallas Cowboys. In college games the same discretion also seems to be used on cheerleader shots.

But, wow! At the Super Bowl the stage was full of beautiful young women in short skirts shaking their rears and humping the air. Does this not provide a certain cache for such behavior to be emulated by the estimated 14 million young people watching the show? Yeah, we've got to do that at our next game!

In Tagliabue's apology about Janet Jackson's exposed bosom, it would seem the entire performance was a total surprise to him. The idea NFL and CBS executives did not watch Super Bowl half time rehearsals is just roll-on-the-floor laughable.

To be fair, the raunchy trend in television, over-the-air and cable, cannot be laid at the NFL's door. ABC's "NYPD Blue" this week announced it might cut a sex scene from a future program. After years of nothing left to the imagination on "Blue," isn't that sweet?

It was watching "Blue" that I first heard on TV the cliché reference to a male's sex organ as his "johnson." Now on the sitcoms and other programs it's johnson this and johnson that.

NBC's "Law and Order," which shows in this market at 8 p.m., is not so graphic with the sex scenes but seems to have no boundaries for inappropriate language.

It is my hope Chairman Powell and the Federal Communication Commission will not issue a censorship rule regarding obscenity on television, thus leaving the FCC staff to decide what is naughty and what is nice.

Powell can get an agreement from TV moguls to clean up programming and set large fines for indiscretions. Unlike film studios and movie theatres, our federal government allocates the right to do programming on TV and radio, thus we have the power to control out-of-control productions.

Two years ago I wrote a guest column for the Star bemoaning the situation where our youth are learning their history from such films as "Pearl Harbor" and "JFK," which do not come near following the facts of these events.

The 2004 Super Bowl show just opens one more door for our young people to feel free to do what seems to indicate approval by our society.

Postscript: On Thursday, May 3, 2005, ABC and other media reported the Texas House of Representatives voted 85 to 55 to approve a bill forbidding sexy cheers and giving the Texas Education Agency authority to punish schools allowing "overtly suggestive" routines at football games and other events. Wow, do I have foresight or what?

Military/National Security

The U.S. Veterans:
Promises Made, Promises Broken

"To care for him who shall have borne the battle and for his widow and his orphan."
— *President Abraham Lincoln, March 4, 1865*

Whether you personally support or disagree with President Bush's threats to militarily conquer Iraq, every citizen should be looking at a "hidden" cost of this war that in time will run into trillions of dollars and continue decades after the guns are silent.

This will be the price for taking care of our military veterans, and their dependents, who may lose life or limbs, be affected by biological warfare or, God forbid, suffer from radioactivity.

My guess is at the White House the entire focus is on, first, winning the war with Iraq and, second, governing a defeated enemy nation as we have with Germany, Japan and, to some extent, Afghanistan.

For any American serving in the military now or who will be in the future, it may be helpful to look at how veterans currently are being treated.

On April 6, 2002, The New York Times reported eligible vets going to a VA medical center near St. Petersburg, Fla., will not be getting their first appointment with a doctor until October, 2005.

Do the math. That would be a wait of more than three years.

And a few months ago on Jan.17, 2003, the Star reported the VA is suspending medical care for higher income veterans with non-service connected ailments.

Florida obviously has many retirees and thousands of vets among them. So let's focus on Arizona and the treatment of vets in this area.

In November, 2000, a local veteran wrote to the VA regional office in Phoenix seeking compensation for a service-connected health problem.

The VA says it usually handles such claims in 8 to 12 months. But this vet's case now is well into its third year with no resolution by the Phoenix office.

On another issue, a veteran was given a year from August, 2001, to August, 2002, to provide medical records supporting the claim he was due compensation for problems related to a surgical procedure while on active duty.

In March of last year, the veteran submitted some 60 pages of medical records going back 35 years to support his claim. But in October the VA sent him a letter saying the case was closed because he had not responded within the one-year period.

The vet then drove to the VA office in Phoenix to look in his file for the medical records he had submitted. They were there, arriving well within the one-year time frame he had been given.

Several weeks later he received a call from the Phoenix office saying his file had been searched, and the 60 pages of records had not been found.

Isolated cases? Not at all, according to Congressman Jim Kolbe's Tucson office where his case work helping veterans is done.

Currently there are 6.8 million American veterans enrolled in the VA system with a budget of $63.6 billion to service their problems.

If you think the VA with this budget is adequately serving veterans, then look at the monthly magazines published by the American Legion, Disabled American Veterans and the Veterans of Foreign Wars.

All are consumed with complaints about the lack of funds and assistance to veterans by our federal government, which seemingly has no end of funds to send young men and women into battle.

The long war in Vietnam produced many thousands of veterans with a new set of health problems including Agent Orange and Post Traumatic Stress Disorder.

Now Vietnam veterans are reaching the ages when the old body begins to fall apart, and for many only the VA offers a way to meet health care and other costs.

President Bush the Elder's massive mobilization for Operation Desert Storm added thousands to the creaking and groaning VA compensation and health care system, and another new health problem called Gulf War Syndrome.

Whether we go to war with Iraq or not, the mobilization of thousands of troops automatically makes them eligible for VA assistance.

In my opinion, this crisis with the lack of service for vets is not entirely the fault of President Bush the Younger, any other president or any Congress. The responsibility can be laid at the feet of the American people who have not supported Abe Lincoln's concept of how we should be treating "those who shall have borne the battle."

So here is a message for Johnny and Mary—before you come marching home.

If you have just signed up for a four-year tour in the U.S. Armed Forces, then send your letter to the VA right away.

Considering the way the VA is responding to veterans these days, you should be getting an answer about the time you are discharged and becoming new veterans in 2007.

Postscript: This column was written in the weeks before the Bush "shock and awe" attack, which began the war in Iraq. It was never submitted to the Arizona Daily Star because, since several of my columns had mentioned my military service, I thought it might be perceived as self-serving. True, I've had some issues with the Veterans Administration over the years, which actually led to the point of this column—that the pre-war White House and Pentagon were not considering the additional costs of caring for vets from an Iraqi conflict.

On June 24, 2005, the Star carried an Associated Press story with this headline, "VA is $1B in red due to health costs." In the article is this paragraph: "The shortage came to light during a routine budget review. Lawmakers said they are still gathering details, but it appears health care for veterans returning from Iraq and Afghanistan and poor budget forecasting contributed to the problem."

When Terrorists Couldn't
Stop a Wedding

Today, Tuesday, Sept. 11, 2001, was not unlike April 19, 1995, the day the Murrah Building in Oklahoma City was blown up by Timothy McVeigh.

On the day of the Oklahoma City bombing the call came from a friend who was assignment editor for NBC evening news in the Washington, DC, bureau and knew of my Oklahoma roots. This morning, just after I had crawled out of bed and washed the sleep from my eyes, my daughter Camilla called from Boston.

"Dad," she said, "something terrible has happened. Terrorists have flown hijacked airliners into the World Trade Center Buildings. I talked to Jamie (my son, a Washington journalist) on his cell phone and he was headed for the Pentagon."

When I turned on the television in my bedroom, it wasn't long before ABC was showing a burning Pentagon. Had my son gone there before the bombing, or to cover the destruction left from being hit by an airliner? My daughter didn't know.

So I watched on TV the various tragedies for a few minutes. There were reports the capitol in Washington had been bombed and this raised concerns about my son's fiancée, Jessica, who works for a New Jersey congressman. After dating more than six years, James and Jessica were to be married Saturday afternoon at Woodlawn Plantation near Mount Vernon.

I turned off the TV, ate an orange, and went out to my front yard to trim the crepe myrtle.

While I was gardening my sister who lives in the neighborhood called and left a message telling me to start watching TV if I did not know what was happening. She was crying and with some reason: her youngest son is deputy assistant secretary for Latin America at the State department in Washington and his wife is in charge of State department overseas assignments. There also were TV reports about a bombing at State.

I grabbed a diet Coke and walked to her home. She and her husband greeted me, both still very upset. I gave her a big hug and said this:

First, if we really believe in God then in these times when we are tested we should have faith that He will see us through this ordeal. Second, since we know many terrorist organizations have the funds and access to nuclear weapons, we should be thankful New York and DC are not just radioactive ruins with millions of people dead including our loved ones.

Back at my home by around 10:30 a.m. Tucson time, I reached my son at his home office. He was on deadline writing an article about the Pentagon bombing, and assured me all was well including his fiancée, Jessica, who had left her House office building for a friend's home.

Those who know me may wonder why a total news junkie would have such a dispassionate interest about the greatest terrorist act in our country in its history.

There are several reasons why I did not spend the day before my television set.

First, at a very early age I went through a war with the Marines.

Then after going to Washington in January, 1961, I had been there through the Cuban missile crisis, the JFK assassination, the Six-Day War in the Middle East, the riots in Washington and Chicago after Martin Luther King's assassination, the 1968 Democratic National Convention riots in Chicago, and numerous protests in the nation's capital.

If my son had been a victim of the Pentagon tragedy, I would have been devastated but hopefully understanding that neither he nor his assignment editor could have imagined such an awful event had he been sent there to do a story.

When I finally reached him by phone after he had covered the Pentagon bombing, the last question I asked was this: is your wedding Saturday on or off?

"Dad," he said, "you know I have been writing about terrorist activities for much of my career. Their agenda is to totally disrupt everything in our lives. But no terrorist is going to stop our wedding. We are going to be married Saturday and I hope the airlines are flying so you can be there."

In the Oklahoma City bombing our cousin, Claudette Meek, was attending a staff meeting of her savings and loan organization and sitting by a window just above where Tim McVeigh's Ryder truck exploded. She and her secretary, Christie Rosas, were the last two bodies recovered before the building was completely demolished.

Late one night in June, James and I toured the Oklahoma City memorial and saw the chair inscribed with Claudette Meek's name.

Today, both father and son are now mentally battle scarred from having personally witnessed death and destruction. But life always continues after every tragic event, and James and Jessica will be married Saturday.

In the future Sept. 11, 2001 will be remembered by everyone for the death and destruction to a country with the greatest military power on earth that today was unprepared. Sept. 15 will be remembered by my family as a glorious day when two courageous kids would not let the great fear in the Washington, DC area following the terrorist attacks interfere with a long planned wedding.

Postscript: James and Jessica had rented a home in Jamaica for their honeymoon trip, and if they were no-shows there would be no refund regardless of the circumstances. They were to fly via American Airlines from Reagan National Airport in DC after their wedding on Sept. 15. But Reagan was closed to any airline activity for weeks after 9/11.

The airline industry was in chaos, so I spent the entire week on the phone trying to arrange their honeymoon flight from another airport. On Friday before the wedding, I got lucky and reserved two seats for them to leave from Philadelphia the next day after their Saturday night wedding at Woodlawn Plantation near Mt. Vernon. At the same time, I also was trying to get myself on a plane to be there for the wedding since my American Airlines flight to DC had been from Tucson to Reagan National.

At 1 a.m. Tucson time on the day of the wedding, American came through with a seat for me to leave that morning on a flight through Dallas-Ft. Worth into the Baltimore-Washington airport.

Our plane arrived at DFW around noon on a nice day and I went to the gate for the second leg of the flight into BWI. The gate was next to a food court, and I made some casual remark about the weather to an American ground crew guy eating lunch there. He said there was no weather expected around DFW until Sunday night.

But some higher power had other plans.

After a few of us boarded the plane, the captain came on the intercom and said there was weather coming through and boarding would be stopped until the storm passed.

Squall lines are common in the southwest and usually quickly pass. But it was three hours later before we were able to take off. In the wee hours that morning after getting the flight, I had called and arranged for a car and driver to pick me up so I would have room to change clothes in the back seat area. After we landed, I discovered the driver had given up on me and gone home. Fortunately, as I scurried around BWI looking for any kind of transportation, I found a limo driver available to take me on the long ride to Woodlawn several miles south of DC.

When we finally got to Woodlawn, I pointed out the entrance to the plantation but the driver insisted on looking for another driveway. He found it and the limo immediately was surrounded by no less than 20 military troops with weapons drawn. That definitely was not the right entrance to Woodlawn.

So I missed the nuptials, arriving just in time for the wedding dinner. James said he would never forget the work I did in getting the honeymoon flight rearranged for him and his bride, Jessica, and that I had stayed in my pit bull mode to get my own flight to be there for this wonderful occasion for two youngsters who had met at my company's staff Christmas dinner in 1994.

Films such as "Pearl Harbor" and "JFK" Give Future Generations A Fraudulent View of History

No, I was not at Pearl Harbor. Neither were those wonderful people in Hollywood who have brought us the blockbuster film "Pearl Harbor," and that's a damned shame.

On Dec. 7, 1941, I was a little boy who had gone on a Sunday trip with his parents, older brother and sister. As my father drove us down U.S. Highway 183 in Western Oklahoma heading to our home, we heard about Pearl Harbor on the car radio. One of my brothers was with a dive-bomber squadron on the aircraft carrier Saratoga in the Pacific, so the news created a time of great despair for our family.

Since then I have seen countless documentaries about Pearl Harbor and known a few survivors including Brig. Gen. Ken Taylor, USAF (Ret.) who, along with the late George Welch, are represented by actors Ben Affleck and Josh Hartnett in "Pearl Harbor."

Taylor and Welch, young Army Air Corps pilots, were able to get their planes in the air from an auxiliary airfield and shot down the first enemy aircraft for our country in World War II.

They were not wearing Hawaiian shirts as portrayed in "Pearl Harbor" or khakis as shown in an earlier film, "Tora, Tora, Tora." Taylor flew that Sunday morning wearing an Army mess dress uniform, the military equivalent of tuxedoes, which were the clothes he had worn for a Saturday night partying in Honolulu and elsewhere.

On Dec. 7, 1971, the 30th anniversary of Pearl Harbor, I hosted a dinner for Gen. Taylor at the Watergate Hotel in Washington, DC, where I heard his heroic story from him for the first time.

"There were no screaming dogfights with the Japanese pilots," Ken Taylor told us. "As we took off from Wheeler Field they were coming across Oahu facing the rising sun and were just sitting ducks."

In Gordon W. Prange's book, "Dec. 7 1941," Gen. Taylor said there were so many Japanese planes he and Welch fell into a sort of traffic pattern with the enemy aircraft and fired away.

In "Pearl Harbor," Taylor and Welch are shown flying so low in aerial combat scenes they sometimes are dodging the Japanese planes by maneurving their aircraft between two-story military buildings. The computer-generated action is no different from the spaceships in "Star Wars" and similar films.

The shame of this erroneous and misleading portrayal of what President Franklin Roosevelt called "a date which will live in infamy," is that present and future generations are getting their history lessons from fraudulent films such as "Pearl Harbor" and Oliver Stone's "JFK." And these portrayals are so far from the truth no teacher, parent, military historian or political figure ever will be able to set the record straight.

What Hollywood produces is such a powerful medium that all over the world it molds opinions and sets standards perpetuated for generations. One example is the idea in films that for a male or female to be really sexy, an obligatory cigarette must be present.

Ironically, one of the most sacred values for which millions of Americans have fought is the First Amendment—which guarantees freedom of expression in our country. And that freedom gives Hollywood the liberty to manipulate history in any way it wishes for monetary reward.

I wholeheartedly agree with this right. Yet at the same time I do feel Hollywood somehow should be held to the same standard often cited as an abuse of free speech: it does not mean we have the right to cry "Fire!" in a crowded theatre when there is no fire.

It is difficult to predict the long-term negative effects of such historically skewed films as "Pearl Harbor" and "JFK." But I'll be damned if I can see one positive effect these films will have on the minds of our wonderful young people who will be making the decisions for this country for decades in the future.

Postscript: This column was used in the Arizona Daily Star on Sunday, June 3, 2001, shortly after "Pearl Harbor" was released. On May 15, 2005, the Star ran a feature by Lance Gay of Scripps Howard News Service about the spin used by the U.S., Soviet Union, UK and Japan to hide realities of World War II. In this feature Professor Donald Goldstein of the University of Pittsburgh focused on the glaring mistakes in "Pearl Harbor." "They say bad history is better than no history because it gets people interested in reading more about it. But these kids today are not going to the bookstore. I'm teaching and I know it."

Goodbye Darkness, Hello Rain

It all began over the 1981 Christmas holidays when a houseguest left behind a paperback edition of William Manchester's "Goodbye Darkness."

For weeks I had eyed the book suspiciously on the nightstand of the guest bedroom. I am not a Manchester fan. But the brilliant red cover with eagle, globe and fouled anchor, which make up the Marine Corps emblem, enticed me more than once. Then one evening as I hurriedly packed for a trip to Tokyo, I threw the book into my carry-on bag for the lack of anything lighter in weight or heavier in subject.

"Goodbye Darkness," I recalled from reviews, was Manchester's chronicle of a 1979 journey made through South Pacific combat zones where he served as a Marine sergeant during World War II. As Pan Am's 747SP soared along on its 14-hour nonstop flight from New York to Tokyo, I moved through the pages of "Goodbye Darkness" quickly since there was no competing movie in the section of the aircraft where I sat.

As I read, two thoughts grew stronger by the hour.

First was the irony of the title and the facts of the flight. We literally were saying goodbye to darkness. For when we passed over Alaska's Mt. McKinley hours after the noon departure from New York, the day was as bright as it had been on takeoff. The man sitting next to me, an Estee Lauder executive from London, had remarked, "By jove, we'll be all the way to Tokyo and the bloody sun will never go down!" The second thought, which came to me somewhere over Canada, was the possibility of a Manchester-type trip of my own to South Korea where I had served in the 1st Marine Division during that war.

I asked the flight attendant for a better map than the one in the Pan Am magazine and she eventually returned with something.

"This is a real relic," she said. And indeed it was, battered, dog eared, and coffee-stained. I still have it. But it did give me a clear idea of the distance from Tokyo to Seoul, which was near the area some of my service with the Marines. It was about the same flight time as Washington, DC, to Chicago I judged. Then I tucked the old map into my carry-on as a souvenir and went back to following Manchester from Guadalcanal to Iwo Jima.

Except the thought of revisiting Korea would not go away.

It had been, I recalled, almost 30 years since the 1st Marine Division had packed its gear and in cold rain and mud moved from front line positions on the East Coast to a new section above Seoul, the capital. (In checking, I was two weeks off the date.)

What a miserable trip it had been. Huddled together in the rear of a six-by truck, cold, lurching, gears grinding for endless hours. Finally, at the foot of a hill overlooking a valley of rice paddies near Munsan, our truck came to a stop. This would be the new site of the 1st Marine Division hospital where, as a Navy corpsman, I would be in charge of the medical and surgical wards.

If anyone on that day had suggested I would ever want to return there after I left, his life would have been seriously threatened.

So much for anniversaries.

By 10 hours into the flight I discovered there were several people I knew on board, so we talked on to Tokyo and both "Goodbye Darkness" and South Korea were forgotten. Until we landed.

Somewhere in the rush of packing for the trip and attending a wedding for my chief assistant, I had neglected to get a visa for Japan.

The Japanese immigration officials at Tokyo's Narita Airport were polite, of course. But with no visa, there would be no entry to Japan.

A Pan Am official appeared and I was led back to the gate from which I had just left. He understood my situation, he said, and there was a solution.

If I would purchase a ticket to another destination in the area—Seoul, for example—I could stay in Japan for 72 hours. Then, after the trip to Seoul I would have another 72-hour grace period. If I had contacts in Tokyo, the Pan Am agent said, they probably could fix me up with a visa and the side trip to Seoul wouldn't even be necessary.

Out came a credit card and a roundtrip ticket to Seoul was quickly written. No longer was South Korea a thought, it was a near certainity because I knew I could not finish my business in Tokyo in 72 hours.

Having left New York Sunday at noon, it was now Monday night in Japan. My schedule of meetings in Tokyo was not firm at all.

On Tuesday morning I asked my "contact" at Sony to try to get the visa extended to Saturday, when I planned to leave. He said it couldn't be done. I then asked for and was given an immediate appointment with Ambassador Mike Mansfield, whom I had known from the days when he was the U.S. Senate Majority Leader and I was press secretary to one of the most powerful members of that body. After several cups of coffee and remembrances about the Senate, he said the embassy was powerless to help. By then I also had learned my major appointment was Friday. So, I definitely was headed for a one-day turnaround trip to Seoul.

At 5 a.m. Thursday I was up like a Marine boot, dressed, and on my way to Narita Airport. Two hours later we took off for Seoul into a beautiful, near cloudless day. Mt. Fuji rose ahead, its winter gown a white cone almost as majestic as McKinley had been.

That view alone was worth the trip. By the time we hit cloud cover a half hour out of Narita, I already had seen more of Japan than I had on my first visit there in 1951.

We had left Camp Pendleton in September to board the S.S. Marine Lynx at the docks in San Diego. And what a sendoff.

Not only did we have a band playing the "Marine Hymn" but the greatest of all heroes to Marines, Brig. Gen. Chesty Puller, was there to bid bon voyage. Standing on the dock he bantered with the officers on decks below us. I could not hear much of what he was saying. But, as the Lynx moved away from the dock, Chesty yelled one last piece of advice.

"Keep to the high ground, boys," he said.

As the Marine Lynx heaved and humped its way through heavy, stormy seas on a 13-day trip to Kobe, Japan, script was issued to us and a three-day liberty promised before we began our final leg to combat in Korea.

It was here that television evangelist Pat Robertson, a Marine lieutenant, allegedly phoned his father, a powerful U.S. Senator, to use his influence to get him an assignment in a rear echelon unit instead of going to the front line with the other officers.

But the Kobe stopover was not to be. At that time the 1st Marine Division was taking a beating in the hills near an area known in news dispatches as "Heartbreak Ridge." In particular the fighting was heavy for "The Rock," a piece of property about 700 yards from Hill 812. It was an area I would come to know intimately as the hospital corpsman for the third platoon, Baker Company, 1st Battalion, 7th Regiment.

The Division needed help quick. Instead of contributing a good cash crop to the economy of Kobe, Japan the next three days, we left the Marine Lynx troop transport ship, walked across the docks to an armed AKA Navy vessel and headed for Korea in the setting sun.

There were not enough bunks on the AKA so my "bed" became the well of an anti-aircraft gun on deck. It was a big mistake. During the first night there was an air raid and I was thoroughly stomped by a sleepy gun crew before I could scramble out of their way.

The next afternoon we went over the side of the AKA on cargo nets, and into amphibious landing craft. In short time we waded ashore in South Korea.

As replacements, we were scattered to different units to fill the slots of those lost in combat or going home on rotation. A few hours after landing in Korea I said "hello" and "goodbye" to my new platoon leader, a young lieutenant named Eddie LeBaron, who would later quarterback the Washington Redskins. He was being rotated to a job as a forward observer for Marine artillery.

As quickly as possible we were moved to fill slots in frontline units. We said goodbye to our Camp Pendleton buddies and loaded up in trucks for a cold, dusty, miserable ride under booming, cracking, scary-as-hell artillery shelling. Then came the rain, and a long slippery climb that eventually led to the safety of a bunker on top of and slightly down the front slope of Hill 812.

Early the next day, still in a cold rain, I accompanied a squad-size patrol to Hill 673 where some of worst fighting had taken place. The Korean hills normally were covered with tall pines not unlike those you might see in Virginia or Colorado. Nothing was left standing on Hill 673 that was more than two feet tall.

"Keep to the high ground, boys," Chesty had said. But, first, you have to take the high ground. He forgot to tell us that.

In 1951 the rotation system worked well, requiring only a year's duty in Korea. As Marines boarded ship to go home, replacements came and we newcomers gradually worked our way from frontline units to rear echelon jobs.

Thus, after duty with a mortar company and the battalion aid station I eventually was assigned to the 1st Marine Division hospital. It was a M*A*S*H unit without Hotlips Houlihan other female.

About the same time I was assigned to the hospital there also came from God knows where a new commanding officer.

The new C.O. was a navy lieutenant commander and, of course, a doctor. He was short with black hair and a mustache reminiscent of Der Fuhrer.

As noncombatants, some of the Navy doctors felt they had to somehow be more macho than the Marines whose job it was to do the fighting. Commander McKay (not his real name) was one of these. He instantly earned the nickname, "Black Mac."

A little scene with Black Mac was the only time in five years of active duty I ever even remotely thought of hitting an officer. And it was all over Marilyn Monroe.

Not long after the famous nude color photo of Miss Monroe appeared on a calendar, a frontline Marine received one by mail from his brother-in-law in Los Angeles. A few days later while the North Koreans pounded our lines with thousands of artillery rounds, this Marine absorbed a lot of shrapnel in his body.

His condition was serious, but not so much that he forgot to grab the priceless Monroe calendar as he was being evacuated to our hospital.

After most of the shrapnel was removed he was assigned to my surgical ward where the calendar soon appeared on the tent wall behind his cot. God, it was beautiful. Any one of us would have killed for that calendar. Morale on the ward soared.

Black Mac made the rounds of the hospital wards once a week with me at his side. When he came to the cot where the Marine lay swathed in bandages in front of Marilyn Monroe, he exploded.

The picture was disgusting, he said, and did shame and dishonor to the Corps. He ranted on and on. And in his rage he grabbed the calendar from the tent wall and ripped it to shreds.

I stood there in shock. The wounded Marine was crying, both from Black Mac's verbal abuse and his irreparable loss. Even today I can remember how I shook with rage as I witnessed the total stupidity of that scene.

It seemed then that I could never forgive Black Mac. But, I suppose in war as with love all things are possible.

A few weeks after the calendar incident a Marine sergeant in the combat zone went "ape," as mental flipouts then were called. Exactly what happened we never knew, but we were told the sergeant stole a jeep and headed north up the road past our own front line. It took only a round or two of enemy artillery to zero in on the jeep, and it was shortly blasted off the road with a dead sergeant. As soon as it was feasible, a platoon went out to get the body and there were more casualties.

Wounded from the Marine ("We always bring back our dead") platoon and the dead sergeant were brought by helicopter to our hospital. The wounded went to surgery and the sergeant went to the morgue, where Black Mac and I had to certify his death.

A Marine from the sergeant's unit soon appeared with the dead man's gear and told us he was married with two small children.

This made it all the more tragic. Since the sergeant had, in fact, committed suicide, the $10,000 insurance policy carried by all servicemen would be voided. In 1952, $10,000 was a lot of money to a war widow with two kids.

The hospital executive officer came in with the death certificate to fill in the cause of death.

"What'll it be, Sir?," he asked.

Without hesitation, Black Mac looked up from the dead sergeant and faced the exec with the poised pen.

"Killed in action, in the line of duty," he said, and stalked out of the tent. Black Mac did have a heart, if no eye for the naked charms of our beloved beauty.

Unfortunately, on my flight to Seoul the cloud cover over the Sea of Japan continued all the way to Korea and I saw none of the country until we were about 100 feet off the runway at Kimpo Airport. It was not the same military airfield I had left one hot August day in 1952. Today, it was a very modern facility though obscured by that same cold, driving rain.

Since all I had to do was to go through Korean immigration and wait until the 6 p.m. flight back to Tokyo, I found a taxi driver who understood a little English and hired him for the day.

Because of the rain and the low cloud cover, it was difficult to tell just how much Seoul had changed until I reached the center of the city. Then the progress was obvious.

There were only two sites I distinctly recalled. One was a government building I seemed to remember being "the Palace." In 1952, it was battered by the battle the Marines had waged through the city after their amphibious landing at Inchon, a few miles away. I couldn't find it in modern Seoul.

The second landmark was the Chosun Hotel, then a tiny rest and recreation facility operated by the U.S. military.

In the 1st Marine Division at that time there was only one way to get the dream "rest and recreation" in Japan. It was to be both wounded and to earn a Silver Star for gallantry. Lesser recognition earned one night in the Chosun Hotel, and eventually my turn came.

After the usual dusty, bouncing six-by truck ride from Division headquarters to Seoul, I was given a room with a bed and sheets. That in itself was a little bit of heaven.

We were free to go anywhere we wanted in the Seoul-Inchon area, but there really was no place to go. So I went out on the street to walk around.

Just before I came to a jewelry shop (such as it was), the door opened and out walked the "Dragon Lady" straight from the "Terry and the Pirates," comic strip. Milt Coniff could not have drawn her better.

She wore a black silk dress slit from hem to hip of her left leg. Her hair, too, was silky black and tied in a bun at her neck. In high heels, her every step brought the revolving movement of her buttocks under the silk that was blindingly sexy. Having seen no woman in months except the wizened grandmothers who worked the rice paddies near Munsan I could not believe what I was seeing as I followed her down the street. It was magical to watch.

I fell in love. It was, however, a brief affair. Half a block or so down the street she stopped suddenly to look into the window of another shop. In doing so her face turned slightly to the right toward me and she was the ugliest woman I had ever seen. The joke was too cruel for my love-starved, broken heart to believe. I went back to the Chosun and sacked out.

Today, the Chosun has changed as dramatically as the "Dragon Lady" had from rear to front. It is a huge modern hotel with marbled lobby and golden staircase rails. The doormen wear splendid red uniforms and helmets that seem a cross between the Queen's palace guards and a Shogun warrior.

I sipped a martini in the lobby bar and watched American businessmen scurrying about waiting for the rain to stop. And I realized many things can change in 30 years, even where there has been a terrible war.

Before heading north toward Munsan, I stopped at another hotel. It was even more opulent and the shopping arcade beneath it was as nice as any I have ever seen and much better than most—even in Paris.

But there were some surprises.

First, it was difficult to find anyone to speak English. Second, even though I visited several bookshops I could find nothing about the Korean War where I had given that valuable year of my life. And, finally, I could find no one who would discuss the war.

"War? What war?" Even my taxi driver did not remember.

He did remember the route to Munsan and we soon began splashing our way north through the city to the more open country and the rice paddies beyond.

The cold rain was not going to quit. So when we approached the first of several roadside war memorials, I asked him to pull over and stop.

I recognized the colored plaque, much the same as the cover of "Goodbye Darkness." It was in recognition of both the U.S. Marines and their Asian counterparts, the Korean Marine Corps. The KMC, like the Turks who came with the United Nations forces, were the tough kind of people you wanted to have on your flanks when the North Koreans or Chinese decided they needed more real estate to the south.

Driving on north there were some modern homes, school children walking happily in the rain, and lonely pines bringing back memories of those frozen, snow-covered hills to the east in the winter of 1951-52.

Finally, we were at Munsan. There was the valley stretching wide from where our hospital had been against a hill, to the rice paddies and on to more hills. Somewhere in the middle of the valley had been the shower tent. We walked there each day chatting with the Mama-sans and Papa-sans who worked their fields of rice, war or no war. I crawled out of the taxi, standing a few minutes as the rain soaked through my raincoat and jacket. A tour bus passed on the way back to Seoul from a trip to Panmunjom, where the Korean War ultimately had ended.

I got in the taxi and headed for the airport. In Seoul the rain had all but quit and the streets were full of young people, mostly university students. However, scattered among their ranks were a number of young men with camouflage-type shirts and pants but no hats or caps. I wondered if they were some kind of special militiamen, but my driver seemed not to understand when I asked about them.

By the time the taxi dropped me in front of Korean Air Lines at Kimpo, I had decided this whole trip was a real bummer. I should have taken my side trip to Hong Kong or Bangkok.

Why had I forgotten the visa, such a routine matter for a person who traveled the world? And then ended up where I spent a year of my life in what has now been called "the forgotten war." And those thoughts could go on and on as the memories of the dead and wounded I had seen and treated passed once again through my mind and into my heart.

Through all this cold and miserable day, not one person had I been in contact with in Korea would admit there had been a war, or acknowledge that more than 50,000 Americans had died there to keep their country free.

As the KAL A300 took off from Kimpo and punched its way through the dark gray clouds toward Tokyo, my mood lifted with it. My wet raincoat was stowed in the overhead compartment and my jacket and shirt were drying fast. A friendly flight attendant was generous with a good bourbon that had been available only to Marine officers, and not us grunts, in that cold and sticky mud below 30 years before.

I reached into my bag for the English language newspaper I had bought at the Kimpo Airport newsstand. The major story on page one was the amnesty that South Korean President Chung Doo Hwan had granted to 2,863 political prisoners on the first anniversary of his inauguration. There also was a picture. It showed young Korean men in camouflaged shirts and pants rushing to freedom through prison gates. They looked very happy. They had still looked very happy enjoying their new freedom when seen on the streets of Seoul an hour before as I returned to Kimpo Airport.

Ah, freedom. That's why old Harry Truman had sent us to this faraway land. To preserve freedom for a people who had been oppressed by one country or the other for centuries. A little freedom. One way or the other, I guess that's what my year there had helped buy.

I lifted my glass for a toast. Here's to you, Black Mac, you old son-of-a-bitch, wherever you are.

And goodbye darkness, hello rain.

Postscript: This article was written in the spring of 1982 for The Washington Post's Sunday magazine and rejected. I don't know why, but I do know when it is said the Korean War is "the forgotten war" it is the forgotten war.

Oops! Inspector Clouseau Is Back Again

Oh, Peter Sellers, do I ever miss you and Inspector Clouseau and those great "Pink Panther" movies. But, even though you are gone we will have forever the Central Intelligence Agency, CIA, to amuse us with its bumbling, sometimes less than amusing ways.

The CIA is the overseas spy agency for our nation's government. I tell you this upfront because, having taught at Pima Community College the last two years, you may be assured not everyone is clued in on this development.

As our government's spy operation, the CIA is in a difficult position. We get to blame it for everything that goes wrong, such as 9/11, and sometimes the blame is well placed.

Perhaps its best known fiasco was the Bay of Pigs invasion of Cuba in 1961 by exiled Cubans living in the U.S. Having given his final approval of the plan, President Kennedy bravely went on national television and accepted responsibility for this colossal intelligence idiocy. In secret, he probably wanted to send the warplanes, once intended for the invasion's air support, to drop a few bombs on the CIA headquarters in McLean, VA.

We've also learned since 9/11 that Osama bin Laden and his terrorist organization were created by the CIA to fight the Russians in Afghanistan. Then, the monster turned on his master and we now send our young military men and women and spend billions to undo what the CIA created.

In the meantime, we have had five months of around-the-clock media coverage out of Afghanistan about our war there. From what we've seen, could someone please explain why we should have cared if the Russians or the Martians took over this wretched piece of real estate?

However, in fairness it is near impossible for the CIA to take credit for operations that do succeed. Talking about successes would compromise what the agency is all about—secrecy.

About 25 years ago, though, the CIA decided it would join the real world and created a public relations operation. I believe the first head of CIA PR was a retired Navy captain not in the habit of revealing secrets, nor was he considered the brightest star in the Washington, DC, PR world. His successors, I'm told, also have not come from the supernova.

Stay with me, I'm getting to the point. I would like the current CIA PR person to explain to us the absolute and total stupidity of planting bugs throughout a Boeing 767 being outfitted as the "Air Force One" for President Jiang Zemin of China.

Duh.

This is a buggy world. Washington Redskins owner Dan Snyder recently was accused of bugging phones used by his coaches and players. Ken Lay, the former Enron CEO, must have had his office swept by debuggers five times a day.

But for the CIA to think the Chinese are so stupid they would not expect that in the Boeing 767 300ER's 117 miles of wiring bugs would be planted, truly is to believe Osama bin Laden is the Tooth Fairy.

Let's approach this for a moment as ignorant, ordinary persons who are not up to speed on the latest high-end electronic bugging equipment. So let's say the bugs were planted in the aircraft and not found by the Chinese.

Bugs actually are little radio stations that transmit the sounds they receive. When the Nixon campaign planted such devices in the national Democratic headquarters at the Watergate in 1972, the bugs transmitted to a receiver just across Virginia Avenue to a guy listening with a tape recorder in the Howard Johnson Hotel.

Are we now to believe that the bugging state-of-the-art is such that the transmitters allegedly planted in President Jiang's personal jet would transmit hundreds or thousands of miles to where some U.S. cat with a tape recorder would receive these messages?

Get outta here. Even for a government that has paid $500,000 for a single fax machine, we are smart enough to know planting those bugs on the Chinese airplane ranks right up there with the Cuban fiasco.

Don't get too anxious waiting for an explanation from the CIA. It if ever comes it most likely will be a fairy tale story like this. "Oh, a CIA spokesperson said today, "I'm sure the listening devices were there so if the wiring broke there would be a 'pop' heard in the cockpit."

This week a former CIA agent is making the rounds of television talk shows promoting his new book. He said on one program he estimates the CIA budget to be $30 billion annually with most of it just frittered away.

With that kind of money, why didn't the CIA just give President Jiang a new 767, 777 or 747? Why not. Back in the Mideast oil heydays, one American corporation gave a Saudi prince a refurbished four-engine DC-8 jetliner as a Christmas present.

As part of the entertainment center on this luxurious aircraft, the CIA also could have provided a complete set of the Nixon White House tapes. Yo, spooks. You want to really bug a foreign head of state who is not exactly our best friend, then why not go all the way.

Postscript: There is an aged saying that just because you're being paranoid about something doesn't mean in some situations you shouldn't be.

This column was used in the Arizona Daily Star on Feb. 18, 2002. But by then the aftermath of 9/11 had brought about many changes in our lives, especially air travel.

Just a few days before 9/11, I observed—make that celebrated—my 71st birthday.

Before moving to Arizona, I had not traveled less than 100,000 miles annually for years. After moving here, I was not on a plane more than three or four times a year.

But when I did fly, I became the "target" every time for the most thorough scrutiny by the so-called airport security people. Two examples.

The weekend before the 2002 Olympics opened in Salt Lake, I went there for the annual meeting of the American Alpine Club. Though I usually rent a car when I travel, this time I took a bus from the Salt Lake airport to the Snowbird Ski Resort where our meeting was being held.

Returning to the airport on Sunday to fly United back to Tucson with a change of planes in Denver, my companions on the bus were some of the greatest mountain climbers in the world. I doubt any one of them was even half my age

When the bus stopped the terminal and we were getting off, the security people were at the curb. Every other passenger was completely ignored. They were waiting for me and swabbed my hands with cotton that would indicate I had been handling explosives.

Once inside the airport, I again was pulled aside. My hands were swabbed the second time, shoes came off, pockets turned inside out, wand run over all my body, the works. Again, the other climbers—some from other countries—went sailing through security.

Second incident. In August, 2002, I flew down to Auckland, New Zealand, to interview Sir Edmund Hillary, the first person to step on top of the world when he reached the summit of Mt. Everest.

Starting out in Tucson, I got the "full Monty" from the security clowns. But it was the trip back that was a true wonder.

I had flown American from Tucson through Dallas and back to Los Angeles, because it has no direct service from Tucson to LA. For the round trip from LA to Sidney and Auckland, I was booked on Qantas.

After I cleared customs and immigration on my return trip, I went to the American terminal to board the flight to Dallas. To my surprise, the aircraft was a 777 fully booked at 285 passengers. I was the only person of 285 pulled aside behind a curtain and given everything except a prosthetic exam.

It was a long time afterwards that the thought came that this extraordinary treatment might have been from the local FBI office sending my CIA column on to its rabbit warrens in the J. Edgar Hoover Building in Washington, DC.

Probably not. In the meantime the late Gov. Joe Foss, a Marine ace and Congressional Medal of Honor recipient in World War II, was given a major shakedown at the Phoenix Sky Harbor airport because security screeners were suspicious—so help me, God—because old Joe was either wearing or carrying his Medal of Honor.

While I was putting together these columns for this book in February, 2005, Bob Schieffer, host of "Face the Nation" on Sunday mornings, made the same comparison of Inspector Clouseau and the CIA.

Bob, be warned. Get ready to go through the "Full Monty" on your future flights.

The NASA Shuttle Program: Fix the Problem, Not the Blame

The Tucson area has an abundance of people from various disciplines who are especially qualified to write about the Columbia shuttle disaster.

Bob Sirling, the greatest of all aviation writers, and Richard Threlkeld, the former CBS correspondent, come to mind. Then there are dozens of University of Arizona faculty and staff who have in some way contributed to the nation's space effort over the years.

In fact, I believe I am correct in saying the original Mercury Seven astronauts came to the University of Arizona to study the heavens from the Steward Observatory on campus.

But I also have had a little experience with our space program and it is for this reason I want to share a story relating to the crisis presented by the Columbia's unfortunate demise.

It's a crisis because we have U.S. astronauts aboard the space station orbiting above us every day, and because it should be a given that our space program must move ahead at top speed.

The question is, without knowing if we ever will find the definitive answer to the Columbia's last minute breakup, should we move ahead more or less on schedule?

But, first, let's go back to the early days of our space program.

In January, 1961, I left Tulsa to become press secretary to the late U.S. Sen. Robert S. Kerr (D-OK), who was taking over as chair of he Senate space committee.

When President Kennedy went looking for a new person to head the National Aeronautics and Space Administration (NASA), Kerr quickly put forward the name of James Webb, a top executive at the Oklahoma City headquarters of Kerr-McGee Oil Company, which the senator had founded.

Webb immediately was dubbed a crony of Kerr, an oil millionaire never popular with the national media. Few bothered to look at Webb's credentials.

He had been budget director for President Truman, undersecretary of State, and a genius at public administration and Washington politics.

But before Webb hardly had learned where to find his office at NASA, President Kennedy went before a joint session of Congress in May, 1961, asking for approval and funding for U.S. astronauts to go to the moon and back in that decade.

Under Webb's leadership NASA went from failures to success with the inaugural flights of Alan Shepherd, Gus Grissom and John Glenn.

From the Mercury program we went to the Gemini flights then to the Apollo 11 success that put U.S. astronauts on the moon on July 25, 1969, some six months before the end of the decade.

My last involvement with the space program was serving as public relations consultant to the Synthesis Group, a space study commission headed by then Vice President Dan Quayle and my fellow Oklahoman, Astronaut Tom Stafford.

During that time I went to see Jim Webb, severely ill with Parkinson's Disease and not long from his death.

"Mr. Webb," I said, "considering the complexity of all the spacecraft built by the lowest bidder, weren't we awfully lucky to have put our astronauts on the moon with all returning safely?"

"John," Mr. Webb answered in a quavering voice, "there is no one on earth with an imagination that could comprehend the complexity of our trips to the moon, and how very lucky we were to pull it off."

Lucky. Yes. But according to the late Julian Scheer, long time NASA public affairs officer, when I interviewed him two years ago, our astronauts never would have made it to the moon without Webb's skillful leadership as NASA's administrator.

Chances are we will never know what among infinite possibilities exactly what went wrong with the Columbia.

But our work in space must go on without delay.

With the Challenger it was the "O" rings. With Columbia it might have been the tiles. Whatever, if I were an astronaut scheduled to be a crewmember on the next scheduled flight, I would take the same position I did in volunteering for various assignments in the military. I would say, "Let's roll."

Postscript: In the evening of May 15, 2005, one of the cable channels in the Tucson area ran a NASA documentary about all the testing done since the Columbia disaster. One of the NASA experts said everything would be done to make the next shuttle flight safe, but that there can never be a complete guarantee that something so complex as a shuttle flight cannot go wrong. Just echoing Jim Webb.

My Time with The Wall

After Jan Scruggs conceived the idea for a memorial in Washington, DC honoring all Vietnam War veterans, I was invited to lunch one day by the late Frederic (Rick) Hart, a young local sculptor. Rick eventually gained world-wide acclaim for his Ex Nihilo, the sculptures gracing the west front of the Washington National Cathedral, the statue of The Three Servicemen now part of the Vietnam Veterans Memorial, and other notable works.

At the time I headed the Washington office of a major international public relations firm, and Rick wanted us to provide pro bono services to help raise funds for building the Vietnam Memorial.

I agreed, but somewhere my offer of services was lost in miscommunications. But in short time our firm was retained on a fee basis.

This is not the place to tell the near miracle story of how something like an $11 million fund was raised and The Wall built in two years, even though opponents of the Maya Lin design included the White House, the secretary of the Department of Interior which owns the Mall where The Wall was built, powerful members of Congress, numerous military service organizations and one of the country's richest and most successful business executives.

The Wall was dedicated on Nov. 13, 1982. In 2002, Jan Scruggs decided there should be a substantial 20-year observance of the most visited (three million annually) outdoor war memorial in the nation's capital.

There is no doubt but that The Wall has been one of the greatest factors in the healing process created by divisions over the Vietnam War, which ran from 1959 to 1975—longest conflict in our nation's history.

After all these years I still serve as a pro bono public affairs advisor to the Vietnam Veterans Memorial Fund which built The Wall. For the 20th anniversary, I was asked to write a brief personal remembrance for posting on the VVMF anniversary Web site. This piece later was used in the Arizona Daily Star, the Bradenton, FL Herald and, I'm told, other publications.

For this book, I dedicate this remembrance of my time with The Wall to Terry McCann's brother, Lance Cpl. Jimmy McCann, and 2nd Lt. Jay McKeon, brother of my friend, Lollie McKeon, both natives of Chicago with their names etched on The Wall. I never knew Jimmy and Jay. But as three who served in combat with the Marine Corps we are forever brothers-in-arms and lovers of a great city.

Looking at The Wall at
20 . . . and Beyond

When people gather to observe the 50th anniversary of the dedication of the Vietnam Veterans Memorial in November, 2032, it will not be an altogether joyful sight. Even the youngest of those serving in the military when the war officially ended in 1975 will be in their mid-70s.

They will come to The Wall in wheelchairs and leaning on canes, white of hair, unsteady of step, and with faded eyes and fading dreams.

Yet, it should be a glorious day.

Long forgotten will be the raging controversy over Maya Lin's brilliant black granite design.

While lasting no more than a year, only a few of those closely involved know just how intense this battle became behind the scenes with powerful people in the White House, Department of Interior, Congress and the private sector determined the black granite wall never would be built. But in the winter of 1982 a compromise was reached to add a statue and flagpole so construction on The Wall could begin.

Bulldozers raced to the Mall to start moving earth and a groundbreaking ceremony hastily planned before those opposed to the Lin design could come up with a new strategy to stop the project.

Ironically, it was Rick Hart, the statue sculptor, who first asked me to become involved in Jan Scruggs' effort to build a memorial. But it took me years to accept the addition of Rick's statue and other changes to the Memorial site.

Maya Lin had won the world's largest design competition hands down. While I thought the Hart sculpture of the three soldiers a true masterpiece, it just did not seem fair.

Nevertheless, with my son, James, a high school student whose hobby was the Vietnam War, I went to Hart's downtown DC studio on weekends and helped form the clay for the heroic-sized sculpture. My job was to pour liquid plaster into a form that produced rounds of ammo for the bandolier worn by one of the men.

But the truth is Maya Lin simply chose the wrong design competition for a memorial in the wrong city at the wrong time.

Washington, DC, is a place where not even the President of the United States gets 100 percent of what he wants. Over the years, I eventually concluded, why should Maya Lin be any different just because she was a brilliant artist? After seeing the Memorial's tremendous success after the first 20 years, anyone—including Maya—who still has a problem with the compromise should get a life.

In the first 20 years of the Memorial I spent thousands of hours working for VVMF, primarily as a public affairs advisor. Controversy, sadly, did not entirely end with the Nov. 13, 1982, dedication.

In my bookcase is a big hunk of silver and wood, a Public Relations Society of America's "Oscar," which recognizes my small contribution to this effort.

Of course I'm proud of it. But I cannot honestly say it means more to me today than having helped Rick Hart make the bandolier.

Perhaps in the end those gray plaster rounds of ammo were important in bringing closure for me, to cast away the once repugnant idea of powerful politicians messing with something a young Yale architecture student had won fair and square under the rules.

Whatever it might have been, I'm glad something within led me to let it go—just as The Wall has helped so many affected by this long and terrible war release their own demons to the stars that shine each night over this wonderful Memorial.

Ex-Marine Shares Sense of
Duty Felt by Fallen Heroes

It's more than 2,500 miles or whatever the AAA roadmap says is the distance between Bradenton, FL and Green Valley, AZ, a retirement community 25 miles south of Tucson.

Green Valley is a conservative area, ever swelling with retired military men and women.

But tonight, across this great stretch of America from Arizona to Florida, I feel your pain.

Tonight "The NewsHour with Jim Lehrer," as it often has five nights a week for months, showed in silence the photographs and identity of 18 servicemen killed in Iraq. Somewhere about in the middle of names was Marine PFC Christopher R. Cobb, 19, of Bradenton.

I looked at his young face and thought of all the family and friends who are grieving his loss.

It took me back to a time as the Christmas holidays approached in 1950. I was in the Navy in the San Francisco Bay area and, out of nowhere, selected to escort the body of a sailor from the Korean War for burial in St. Petersburg.

In Ohio a blizzard hit so furiously it stopped our train in Cincinnati, so I sought refuge for the night at the local YMCA. When I walked into the train station the next morning, MPs, Navy Shore Patrols and local police descended on me like a mountain avalanche.

At the time, no serviceman's body could be moved while traveling without the escort being present to—in this case—see the casket transferred from one train to another. So two trains had been sitting there waiting for me.

It didn't get any better in St. Pete. The sailor's parents were divorced and I was faced with the decision about who—father or mother—would receive the flag draping the coffin at the end of the service at the cemetery. I chose the mother, and the father graciously understood.

The family, Cuban Americans, wanted to adopt me. What no one knew was that I very much wanted to go to Korea as a medical corpsman with the Marines, and these nice people did not need another sailor to worry about.

By summer I was training with the Marines at Camp Pendleton. In September, 1951 we landed in Korea, where I served most of a year with the same unit to which PFC Cobb belonged at his death—the 1st Marine Division.

To close this circle, I come back to PFC Cobb.

He, as in my case, was a volunteer for military service. Chances are many of those on the Iraq casualty list mirror my own teen years. No decent jobs after high school, no opportunity for more education and, worst of all, no hope.

One of my longtime friends is Brig. Gen. Ken Taylor, USAF (Ret), now the first living designated and decorated hero of World War II. Ken and a fellow Army Air Corps pilot, Lt. George Welch, were able to get their planes in the air to fight off the Japanese attackers Dec. 7, 1941, at Pearl Harbor.

Last Dec. 7, Ken said on NBC Evening News he took off to face some 300 attacking Japanese aircraft "because I was too young and too stupid" to know the danger he faced.

So was I by volunteering for Korea, and we both lucked out.

If this is any comfort to those who mourn PFC Cobb, it is important to young men to carry out what they feel is their destiny. In doing so some end up with their names on a white cross among the thousands on the rolling green turf of Arlington or other cemeteries.

We know if we fall, left behind will be grief, sorrow, guilt and many regrets. But for those left behind, one would hope they might understand we must follow our hearts for better or worse. And in the case of PFC Cobb, it is a great sorrow it had to be the latter.

Postscript: This column was used Sunday, April 25, 2004, in the Bradenton, FL, Herald. I wrote it after months of watching photos of those military men and women, who have died in Afghanistan and Iraq, shown in silence most evenings at the end of "The NewsHour with Jim Lehrer."

If you think about it, for every one of those who die in this war there are dozens or perhaps hundreds of family and friends to mourn the loss.

But we don't think about just how far this sorrow of losing our mostly young men and women can reach. In most instances, except for a celebrity such as Pat Tillman, the former Arizona Cardinals player who was killed by friendly fire in Afghanistan, after being shown on "The NewsHour with Jim Lehrer" they will never be heard of again except in their own communities.

Somewhere out there I fervently hope there is another Jan Scruggs, who conceived the idea for the Vietnam Veterans Memorial and saw it built, so those names will be etched on a new memorial to be remembered forever by a grateful nation.

Déjà Vu all over Again

For several weeks I have been listening to our generals boast about how quickly U.S. forces can defeat Saddam Hussein and the Iraqi military.

Then on the evening news March 18, about 24 hours after President Bush had addressed the nation and given the Iraqi leader and his two sons 48 hours to leave, the so-called military experts moved from the ridiculous to the sublime.

Two on "The NewsHour with Jim Lehrer" blatantly predicted a war of two weeks duration. Two weeks?

I personally like Tony Cordesman, the veteran military analyst for ABC-TV News. With Tony there is no blow dry hair, contact lens, Chiclets teeth or eye tucks. Just good, hard information. And I can't remember Tony predicting the war with Iraq would be over in a fortnight.

Maybe our military leaders think they are going into Grenada, Panama or Haiti.

More than one military man has said on television he almost wishes Saddam will use some form of chemical warfare, to show the world Iraq indeed does possess the weapons of mass destruction he vows do not exist.

I'm guessing none of these guys, as we used to say in the Marines, are "taking the point" by being in front of all other troops.

As Yogi Berra once said, it sounds like déjà vu all over again.

While a kid, I used to deliver a little weekly national newspaper called Grit. Prior to Pearl Harbor, I remember reading in Grit that some experts were predicting a war with Japan would be over in 30 days.

It is not the 1940s and this time our own nation is the one planning a surprise attack on another country.

But if is true that Saddam Hussein has so many weapons of mass destruction, why will he not use them on our own forces who plan to leave no sand dune unturned until he is killed or imprisoned forever?

We have a great military machine amassed around Iraq. There is no doubt it will move, to paraphrase Julia Ward Howe, as "a terrible swift sword" across a country that in so many ways is already vanquished.

Every president has to trust the military leaders. They are the professionals who assess war situations and present battle plans to the Commander-in-Chief.

Unfortunately, going back many years, George Bush the Elder has been the only president with real combat experience. Even so, like most of us who have served, he likely never knew any more about the war in the South Pacific than the mission of his own squadron.

With my every prayer and wish for our military success in Iraq, there are two things that bother me about the Iraqi war scenario.

The first was a CBS "60 Minutes" program in recent months that reported on the hundreds of documents the Israelis found when they overran Arafat's PLO headquarters.

Most documents seemed to point to Iran, not Iraq, as the most ardent supporter of terrorism.

The second is the fact the same military leaders directing the Iraq invasion are the same ones who were in charge on 9/11.

In spite of all the many military bases within 200 miles of the nation's capital, the Pentagon could not get a single aircraft in the air in time to shoot down one and probably two hijacked airliners headed there to destroy major federal government buildings.

Are you sleeping better at night knowing they may hold the future of our nation in their hands?

Postscript: This column was submitted to the Arizona Daily Star about a week before U.S. Forces attacked Iraq. I was asked to cut it down to around 650 words. By the time I sent it back to the Star, U.S. planes were bombing Baghdad.

The Cuban Missile Crisis:
Our Nation's Finest Hour

U nless you were there at ground zero, you could never understand how it felt to have Soviet nukes aimed at the nation's capital from Cuba. I argue it truly was our nation's finest hour.

Kevin Costner's new movie about the Cuban missile crisis, "Thirteen Days," nor anything on TV or screen can convey the feeling of inevitability we knew for most of those days.

It was October, 1962. A young Capitol Hill aide, I had been drafting letters for my senator responding to constituents who believed charges by the late Sen. Homer Capehart (R-IN) that the Soviets had put missiles in Cuba.

The Kennedy Administration, at first out of ignorance, denied it. With congressional elections underway, it wasn't easy to admit when U2 flights over Cuba found the missiles.

After President Kennedy came on TV Oct. 22 and told the world the U.S. would not tolerate Soviet missiles in Cuba, an eerie quiet settled over the national capital. Everyone knew the first missile would be aimed at us.

What to do?

There was hardly time to even stock a bomb shelter, let alone build one.

Some people had plans. Most made no sense but they didn't care. One neighbor family withdrew all its money from the bank to buy a new car, and planned to just head west.

At work or elsewhere, not one single person was heard to say Kennedy was crazy for standing firm and leading us into a nuclear war. Through news leaks we knew the young president already was at war with his military leaders.

To the contrary, everybody seemed to feel it was time to stand firm. If this meant the end, so be it. And it became a very proud moment for those of us at ground zero. Heads were held high.

Then, it was over. We breathed a big sigh of relief.

Two days later, representing U.S. Sen Robert S. Kerr (D-OK), I was invited to accompany Sen. Margaret Chase Smith (R-ME) on a fact-finding trip to our Navy base at Guantanamo Bay, Cuba.

Marines in fatigues covered practically every inch of the little base. U.S. warships in the bay were anchored so close you almost could walk from shore to shore on them.

After an elegant dinner hosted by the base commander the first night, Sen. Smith and her aide went to their quarters and I went to the officer's club with the generals.

Then I really understood what had been going on at the White House. The generals were unanimous: invade Cuba and to hell with diplomacy.

I tried to talk about the need to have members of the Organization of American States and the United Nations stand with us. The generals laughed.

It was mentioned that with Khrushchev's agreement to remove the missiles, Cuba was not a threat. The generals laughed louder. Having gone through a war with the Marines, I understood. They weren't trained to be diplomats or politicians.

Then I told them how it felt in recent days to be at ground zero in our nation's capital. The bar grew quiet.

Had the military prevailed at the White House, we now know it would have been the end of civilization. Instead, it became our finest hour.

Postscript: The column ran in the Star on Feb. 4, 2001. As close as we came to a nuclear holocaust during the Cuban Missile Crisis, some White House insiders believe we actually were closer to lobbing nukes at each other during the Six-Day War in 1967 between Israel and Egypt. By that time there had been a "hotline" arrangement made between the White House and the Kremlin which was manned 24/7. See more about this situation in President Johnson's "The Vantage Point," chapter 13, p. 187. Holt, Rinehart and Winston, 1971.

Land Mines:
It's Time for Them To Go

Navy hospital corpsman Robert Neary did not have to be with the Marines on Hill 812 that day 50 years ago in Korea.

I don't know how Neary came to be transferred from his Navy duty to the Marine Corps, which has no medical personnel of its own. But I do know that when the Marines found out he couldn't see three feet without the use of his thick glasses, they wanted to send him back to the safety and relative comfort of the Navy. But Neary wouldn't go.

So on a beautiful, cloudless fall day he accompanied a squad of Marines from his platoon on a patrol down into the rocky river bottom that separated Hill 812 from the North Korean forces on the other side.

Early in the afternoon the patrol came under enemy fire. Then a Marine stepped on a land mine, which blew one foot off. Neary, acting as trained, rushed to the aid of the Marine and in doing so stepped on a mine which blew off one of his legs.

Shortly afterwards a few Marines and I, also a corpsman in the same company with Neary, were ordered to take stretchers and race down the hill to rescue the wounded.

We got them on stretchers. I checked the tourniquets the Marines had put on their legs to stop the bleeding, and administered blood plasma and morphine. Through a hail of enemy mortar and small arms fire we carried the wounded back up Hill 812, where they were evacuated by helicopter.

Both men lived and when I finally came home from the Korean War I visited Neary at the U.S. Naval Hospital in Oakland, CA.

This is a war story I have never shared with anyone until now. But today the news from Afghanistan was just too, too much.

It started with "Good Morning America" reporting there are an estimated seven to nine million land mines planted in Afghanistan alone. It ended with Peter Jennings, the ABC-TV news anchor, telling us another U.S. serviceman was coming home from Afghanistan just like Corpsman Neary—without one foot.

When I visited Neary in the Navy hospital, he seemed a little bitter and who could blame him?

Being very lucky, I came home from a year in Korea more or less unscathed. In those 50 years since then I have run marathons, spent hundreds of great days on skis, and played countless games of tennis. Neary probably was never able to do anything like that.

I know much is being done to rid the world of land mines. But if there are a possible nine million in Afghanistan, think about Vietnam, Laos, Cambodia and other countries.

In 1997, the Nobel Peace Prize was awarded in equal parts to the International Campaign to Ban Landmines (ICBL) and to Jody Williams, the anti-land mine campaign coordinator.

From the Nobel Committee's Web site:

"There are at present probably over one hundred million anti-personnel mines scattered over large areas on several continents. Such mines maim and kill indiscriminately and are a major threat to the civilian populations and to the social and economic development of the many countries affected."

Some 1,000 organizations are now affiliated with ICBL but we have to do more, much more, to rid the world of these terrible weapons.

Though not a Vietnam veteran, I have served since its beginning 20 years ago as a public affairs advisor to the Vietnam Veterans Memorial in Washington, DC—the most visited outdoor monument in our nation's capital. And I know how Vietnam and most other vets feel about Jane Fonda.

This is how I feel. If old Jane would put her very substantial fame and fortune behind an effort to ban land mines, I promise you this: Just give me the time and place, Jane, baby, and on behalf of Corpsman Neary, the U.S. serviceman who lost a foot today in Afghanistan and the thousands of other victims of this insidious evil, and I will be there to march with you.

Postscript: This column was in the Arizona Daily Star on Dec. 31, 2001. Today, the effort to find and destroy land mines seems to have been put on the back burner by the media.

Olio (Webster: Olio.
A collection of literary
or musical works.)

If I Can't Understand these Words Then I Must Be Facing Opprobrium

Growing up in a rural community in Western Oklahoma during World War II, I came to idolize Ernie Pyle, the Scripps Howard columnist who was killed while serving as a war correspondent April 18, 1945, on the island of Ie Shima in the Pacific.

I read every word Ernie wrote during the war even though he was never in the areas where members of my family were serving in the military. Then there were his books, and I'm guessing I have read Ernie's "Here Is Your War" 20 times or more.

Ernie Pyle did not write much about generals, his usual subjects being what was then called G.I. Joes. And unlike James Michener, the late noted author and other correspondents who visited my Marine unit during the Korean War, Ernie actually seemed more at home with enlisted men than officers.

He wrote simply and beautifully and I wanted to do the same thing when I grew up.

I enjoy the columnists carried by the Star who, while most friends don't agree with me, provide a balance between the left, right and middle of the road. Surprisingly, because my daughter once worked for her, I have come to especially like Ariana Huffington and the way she cuts to the chase.

Then I read Tom Friedman and Maureen Dowd and wonder if they aren't trying to outdo George Will at being George Will. You know, all those obscure references or quotes from Homer, Disraeli, and Shoeless Joe Jackson.

These folks need a good old Ernie Pyle wakeup call. Here are examples from just one day of the (Arizona Daily) Star's Opinion page on Oct. 17:

Maureen Dowd, writing about what she feels are bumbling attempts by law enforcement officials to catch the Beltway sniper:

"Montgomery County, Md., Police Chief Moose says he's looking for 'closure.' I wish he'd simply look for the sniper.

"Closure is a chimera, if not a canard."

Really, Mo? What ever happened to illusions and lies? George Will would be so proud of you for that line. And jealous.

We go next to Tom Friedman tearing into students who are tearing into those universities that have holdings in companies doing business with Israel.

Tom probably has as many Pulitzer Prizes as Joe Montana has Super Bowl rings. His knowledge of the Middle East no doubt exceeds that of any working journalist, he writes well and speaks even better.

So in this column Tom writes, "Criticizing Israel is not anti-Semitic, and saying so is vile. But singling out Israel for opprobrium and international sanction—out of all proportion to any other party in the Middle East—is anti-Semitic, and not saying so is dishonest."

Opprobrium, Tom? Anybody have a little opprobrium with their oatmeal this morning? Probably not. That would come later on the golf course or, in my case, the tennis court. But it is very, very George Will.

It is said that imitation is the sincerest form of flattery. But, please, Mo and Tom, can't you just go back to using words most of us understand? Who wants to go get a dictionary when we're reading the morning paper over coffee and orange juice. Besides, one George Will is enough already.

Postscript: The Star used this column on Oct. 23, 2002. In May, 2005, Maureen Dowd devoted an entire column to the subject of chimeras.

My Favorite Town Needs
A Miracle Now

For 26 years, I worked in downtown Washington. For 12 years, my offices were in the 1700 block of Pennsylvania Avenue NW. (The White House is at 1600 Pennsylvnia Avenue.) Then, for the last 14 years, they were in the historic Shoreham Building at 15th and H streets NW.

Only a few years ago, my recent move to offices in the more residential Northwest area of DC would have dismayed me. I found it exciting to be downtown, where I could see national sparklies such as Sam Donaldson or Robert McNamara walking to lunch. I was happy in the illusion that I was on the pulse of a world power.

But, I don't think I'll miss being there anymore. Too many things have changed.

For example, last winter I walked the two short blocks from 15th and H to a bank at K Street and Vermont Avenue. The only other people on the street were the homeless. They occupied every bench in McPherson Square. They were asleep in doorways and squatting on the sidewalks, many following me with pleading eyes and outstretched Styrofoam cups.

At least one of the street's regulars always seemed deranged, walking around, yelling his or her rage at the world. This person would be around for a day, for weeks or months before being replaced.

I don't know why any one of these wretched human beings was out on the street, toting a cart full of rolled-up bundles or stuffed plastic bags. But it hurts me in my guts that just in my little corner in the center of our nation's capital, I would see dozens of homeless people, and their numbers seem to be growing each year.

Crime also has become a constant companion downtown. My offices were burglarized three times, the last time on Labor Day 1991. That time, the perpetrator was apprehended by the driver for the Secretary of the Department of Veterans Affairs, which had offices next door. The thief had taken a color TV, walkie-talkies and valuables from a locked file cabinet. He also had trashed the office.

The driver called a VA security guard, who after determining that the stolen goods didn't belong to the government, let the thief go.

More serious is the case of the wife of the owner of a clothing store near my old offices. She was robbed at gunpoint in the middle of the day a few weeks ago. Twice last summer, thieves also broke the store's plate-glass windows.

I won't be missing the 17,000 cars, trucks and buses that passed my office door daily, either. Thanks to the fears generated by the Oklahoma City bombing, my street inherited the Pennsylvania Avenue traffic when the stretch in front of the White House was closed to vehicular traffic to protect the president. Mr. Clinton may be breathing easier because of it, but for us it was like having an office on the shoulder of I-95. The only difference was in the speed of the passing vehicles, not the number.

I also won't miss the trash on the streets and sidewalks, mostly left by visitors who really can't be blamed when the trash receptacles are overflowing. The tourist business pumps $5 billion into our local economy each year, and we can't give visitors a place to toss their candy wrappers.

And do I need to mention that I won't miss the bike messengers? Not long ago I saw one zipping down H Street in the oncoming lane. He was hit by a truck. When the truck driver got out to see how badly the biker was hurt, he was greeted by a string of four-letter words.

In front of our building last spring, another biker was killed when he challenged a taxi going through the intersection.

I hope for a miracle that things will change downtown, less than 100 yards from where the president of the United States lives and works. But for now, like so many other places I've seen, it may be a nice place to visit, but I wouldn't want to work there.

Postscript: This column was in The Washington Post on Sunday, Jan. 5, 1997. Sometimes what we write is topped by a response. As a result of this column, The Post on Jan. 19, 1997 ran one by a man named Marcus Ring, born in 1915, who grew up in the neighborhood near the White House. He and one of his buddies would take President Harding's dog for a walk, and get an ice cream cone reward from the White House cook. Cops chased down speeders in vehicles on Pennsylvania avenue, which passes by the White House, on bicycles.

Let's Quit Messing Around
And Bury the Verb "Lie"

There should be two burial services, one for the New York area and another somewhere in the vicinity of Los Angeles for the Hollywood crowd.

For the East Coast communicators the Meadowlands, home of the New York Giants even though it's in New Jersey, would be ideal and large enough to hold the thousands who would be in attendance. And Jimmy Hoffa, allegedly buried somewhere under the Meadowlands turf, could use some company.

On the West Coast the Los Angeles Coliseum seating 100,000 would be ideal.

These burial services would be for the verb "lie," which is as dead as William Shakespeare whenever I hear the spoken word—most especially on television and in movies.

So now that the mystery of "Deep Throat" is solved, I would like to know just who decided that when there is a line about some resting object the verb "lay" is substituted for "lie."

Once upon a time detectives in a film or television mystery would proclaim, "The body was found lying there near the door." Now, it is just universally accepted that sleuths such as those in "Law and Order" or "NYPD Blue" say, "The body was found laying there near the door."

With no disrespect intended, it's doubtful the majority of cops have college degrees in English. But we get no better grammar from actors playing lawyers, who theoretically have a degree the equivalent of a doctorate in other fields.

I challenge you to listen carefully to newscasts, film and television dialogue and use your thumbs to count the number of times someone uses"lying" instead of "laying" in the proper context.

Once upon a time I took a yellow legal pad and kept score of the times the verb "lie" was misused on television, with the system of four marks with one through them to indicate five points as in some parlor games.

It didn't take long to fill half a page and was no fun doing it anymore.

I have no idea what the system might be at this time, but years ago children playing roles in films didn't get a pass on school. The studio provided tutors to see these child stars such as Shirley Temple learned their ABCs.

Perhaps it would help if movie and television production companies had grammar tutors around to help the stars when they are not in front of a camera. The least the writers could do is have a copy "The Elements of Style" by Strunk and White handy on their desks.

But that's not going to happen so we should go ahead with planning the appropriate burial services, putting "lie" in two little boxes as we do with mementoes in a time capsule.

And after the ceremonies and benedictions at the two burial sites, we should just let sleeping dogs lay.

God Save the Queen . . .
and Forgive Her Trespasses

Pardon me, folks, if I have not had the appropriate celebratory spirit for Queen Elizabeth's 50th anniversary observance. The reason is I think there is something rotten in England.

Queen Elizabeth has had a free ride with the media and her subjects for half a century. What makes her look all the more like Miss Goody Twoshoes is that others in the family have reaped heaps of negative publicity for escapades with their wives/husbands/lovers and otherwise tacky behavior.

It seems to me, though, that the various offspring of Phillip and Elizabeth have had a very unfair deal in life.

It is well known that Prince Phillip has given nothing to his son, Charles, heir apparent to the throne, but scorn and a general back of the hand treatment. What is never considered in the royals watch is that underneath the queen's polished veneer is a really lousy mother.

Let me cite just one example which I think makes my case.

Way back when Charles was just a wee tot, about five years old, the queen went off on a long world tour of what was once the British Empire. In a documentary about the royal family, the queen was shown stepping off the royal yacht upon her return to England.

Little Charlie was standing there all decked out in his Sunday best to welcome mum home. So what does the queen do? She shakes hands with the little dude and moves on to greet others in the welcoming party.

Can you believe it? She shook hands with the kid, who hadn't seen his mother in weeks!

Now there is a lady who needed some serious coaching about rearing children and a figurative kick in her royal behind for being such a poor excuse for a mother. Would it really have severely violated royalty protocol to have picked up little Charlie and given him the big hug he obviously craved?

It is no wonder Prince Charles has given his parents a little payback by spurning his late young wife, one of the great beauties of the world, for the arms of an older woman.

For the way he has been treated by his parents, he should stick it to them again and marry Camilla Parker-Bowles. Go Charlie.

As for the never-ending argument that England needs no royal family, my vote would be for keeping them for all their faults. The pomp and circumstance that go with the royal family is worth billions of dollars to the British economy in tourism.

I have been to London many times, once met Prince Phillip and years ago had a front row seat at the queen's birthday celebration at the Horse Guards compound.

As a country boy from Oklahoma, there is no way England would be the same for me without all that color and pageantry. Not to worry. The royals are in no danger of being put out to pasture.

But let us not get carried away with Queen Elizabeth and Prince Phillip as saviors of mankind. They may be the most famous pair of royals in the world, but any parents who cannot hug their kids have a long way to go to earn even a smidgen of my respect.

Postscript: When I submitted this column to the Arizona Daily Star I was a little outraged.

The blameless way Queen Elizabeth has been treated by the media for many years is an outrage. Do we really live in a world where parents are never assigned just a little responsibility for their children's behavior as they go through life?

Apparently so.

Do you ever watch television? Don't young actors and actresses almost always give credit to their parents when they accept an Oscar or other major recognition? It's the same with NFL football stars and those in many walks of life. "Thanks to my parents . . ."

But what if children take the low road and come from parents who were abusive, negligent, demanding, expecting high achievement—or else? Are parents always held blameless?

No, they are not and should not be completely exonerated from all their children's unacceptable behavior.

I was alone out there in the journalism world when I submitted this column to the Arizona Daily Star. There was nothing but disgusting fawning by all media over the Queen for her 50 years as the reigning monarch of Great Britain.

Jim Kiser, then editor of the Star's editorial page, apparently thought enough of my column to put it to a vote with his staff. The vote was unanimous, the verdict being that no one cared if Queen Elizabeth was one of the worst mothers among royalty in England's history.

Damn, I hated to lose that vote. But on Saturday, April 9, after postponing the wedding a day due to Pope John Paul II's funeral, Charles and Camilla did get married. The queen, I think, did not make the right choice by not attending the wedding. Among "distinguished" guests at the reception was Joan Rivers.

Dispatch from the Desert

When I first moved to Arizona in the fall of 1999, almost every conversation I had with locals for the next month concluded with this statement, "Well, that's the desert for you," they said. Then, I never heard it again.

I came here from a forest so to speak, having lived in a condo on a branch of Rock Creek Park in Washington, DC. Rock Creek runs from near the Watergate Building on the Potomac River for miles up into Maryland. Monster hardwoods adjoined the sundeck of our condo, some rising as high as 50 to 75 feet. Once during a wet snowstorm one of the trees fell over a nearby bridge, smashing its iron rails like straws in a Mickey Dee's Coke cup.

In DC where one end of my condo was on Connecticut Avenue, the traffic noise never stopped, 24/7. Out here in the southern part of the Sonoran Desert, in this group of 325 homes you can hear a cactus pod drop. It took me weeks to get used to the almost total silence and darkness after sunset.

Our wildlife is radically different from that in DC and surrounding suburbs. Years ago it was joked in DC that our raccoons there wore little hardhats and used jackhammers to open the tightest of metal garbage cans.

Here we have white-winged doves so persistent they will work for weeks trying to build a nest up high in flowerpots and garage rafters. Our quail are not the bob white variety with their wonderful calls. They are Gambel's quail with cute little topknots, and make a sound like, "Oh, wow." We also have Gila monsters, pack and kangaroo rats, squirrels, hummingbirds, crows, hawks, wrens, the Gila woodpecker and many other varieties of birds.

To add some stature to my neighborhood, it also is home to two world famous residents—Wile E. Coyote and the Roadrunner.

And we have various species of snakes.

Where I grew up in Western Oklahoma the only poisonous snakes I saw were the water moccasin and the cottonmouth—usually when we were seining a creek for minnows to be used as fish bait.

My first experience with a diamondback rattler was late one day when a man from Cox cable came to wire my house. After he had been here awhile, the doorbell rang and he installer apologized for not being able to complete the connection that day. Reason: there was a small diamondback in the cable box outside the house.

My next encounter was when the student who comes on Saturday to help with the garden rang the doorbell, and announced there was a diamondback curled up underneath my dining room window.

For the second time I called the snakebusters from the local fire department. They were here in minutes, taking the rattler by long tongs. One of them then walked about 50 feet to the arroyo that runs next to my house and let it go. It reminded me of an Oklahoman friend who said when they found a rattler they would take a shotgun, killing and burying it with one blast.

My next experience with a diamondback was more serious. And it has a kind of paranormal twist.

I had bought a nice residence just down the street from where I live and was remodeling it to sell at a later date. One

Saturday the student and I went over to the house to do some painting. I pulled my pickup into the garage and started to the small storage room where I keep the paintbrushes.

Before I could reach for the door handle, I realized I had not remembered to bring the key. Along the garage wall were large cabinets and at the bottom in front of me was a piece of green plastic screen. I heard a little sizzzzzz sound, the kind of noise you might hear from wind blowing through a screen and that day the wind was quite strong.

Just then Jesse, the student, standing at the back of the pickup, yelled, "John! Diamondback!

I quickly jumped back and by then the rattles at the end of the snake's tail were at full speed behind the little piece of green screen—the only thing separating me from what was obviously a large diamondback.

The snakebusters were summoned, but by then the snake had crawled somewhere in the big cabinets. All doors were opened. Not a sign.

Shrugging, one of the firemen said he guessed it was a lost cause and they were leaving.

"Oh, no, you're not," I told him. "You're not leaving me with that big SOB crawling around here."

So the fireman went to the truck and came back with an axe, and began to hack away at the floor of the cabinets. In short order the diamondback was snared and put in a clear, heavy plastic snakebox. I'm guessing they drove up the street and released the snake on state land 50 yards behind my home.

Now, for the paranormal part of the story.

Remodeling of the house started on Sept. 1, 2004. The snake incident was April 16. 2005. In almost eight months there were few days I was not at the house, parked in the garage. Twice I had clutter from the remodeling work removed and, on a weekly basis, we would put some trash in a plastic bag.

No one, not myself, Jesse or the contractors can remember seeing the piece of green screen prior to the day it was the only thing separating me from the big rattler. It had no use, it came from nowhere in the house and was not stored in the garage cabinets. The next time I went to the house it had disappeared. Not into a trash bag and it could not have blown away. There must be an explanation but thus far it still puzzles us.

Last year in Tucson, a man was delivering a pizza to a physician's home one night. A big rattler was coiled by the door and bit him. To save his life, he was given 20 shots of antivenom at $2,000 a pop.

But all is not bad about this snake story. The snakebusters release them because they are important in the food chain to keep rodents and other prey under control. If a vehicle is parked in place long enough, for example, packrats will get into the engine area and chew up the wiring. There was a big packrat nest in my garage cabinet, thus the diamondback came there looking for lunch.

According to a documentary I saw on a PBS station, diamondbacks are nocturnal critters that can sense the warmth of a mouse or rat from about 30 feet. It said they range as far as 20 miles searching for food, but always come back to their den for winter.

A herpetologist at the prestigious Desert Museum just west of Tucson disagrees with the documentary statistics. She says the range for food is more like five miles and the heat sensor about 20 feet.

Unfortunately, we will be seeing more snakes and wildlife here because of the thousands of homes being built all around us.

As they say here, "That's the desert for you."

Postscript: This originally was written as an email to my friends back east to tell them about my new life. It was updated to include my latest experience with a diamondback.

The Jayson Blair Bewitched Project

T he world did not stop recently when a reporter from another newspaper told The New York Times it had a reporter making up stories and using those written by other journalists.

This reporter turned out to be Jayson Blair, a young man whose career path at the Times was nothing less than meteoric.

Blair apparently had the freedom to go wherever he wanted to go and cover mostly page one stories. But he did not go on all these trips. Instead of making trips, he made up stories.

And he was the ultimate in Teflon journalists, with warnings from those editors and associates who saw his faults sliding off his slick persona.

The Blair fiasco has been a major reality check for all media.

This is good. But out here in a land that is inundated with media reports as in no other nation, the Blair affair hardly has been a blip on our radars.

One reason could be an analogy with our initial attack on Iraq. The American public in recent years has had its "shock and awe" by media magicians, which softened us up for the incredible Blair fiasco at the Times.

Previously, errant journalists included Peter Arnett of CNN, Christopher Newton of the Associated Press and Stephen Glass of The New Republic.

"60 Minutes" on Sunday, May 11 rehashed the story of Glass, who was a genius at making up stories out of whole cloth and went to unbelievable lengths to fool those who supposedly were supervising him.

I was visiting Washington, DC shortly after Jayson Blair was exposed for his misdeeds at the Times, and The Washington Post was gloating over the problems of the only newspaper it considerers a competitor.

The Post seems to have forgotten it once had a reporter named Janet Cooke, who was awarded the Pulitzer for a series about a crack baby named Jimmie. The Post should have entered her in the fiction category for a Pulitzer, because little Jimmie did not exist.

Again, the world did not stop because of Janet Cooke.

I think media news readers, viewers and listeners are not unlike military people. Complaining is part of the routine, releasing a little anger when life is frustrating or frightening.

As a former frequent flier it also reminds me of a bad airline trip. On a hot summer day passengers board and the plane heads for the runway. Somewhere out there the captain announces we are going nowhere because there are storm cells in the area of the destination airport.

Passengers have to stay seated, there is nothing to drink, no trips to the lavatories and little air. This goes on an hour, two hours or longer. Finally the captain gets the green light and off we go.

Twenty minutes into the flight the plane levels off. The AC is pumped up and passengers can go to the lavatories. Flight attendants roll the beverage carts down the aisle and we can have a Coke or cocktail.

Two hours later the plane lands. All discomfort from back where we started is forgotten as we head to our homes, business meetings or vacation resorts.

For awhile we will wonder why young Mr. Blair's own editors did not discover his charade, and if there are others like him among the media. But, please, give us credit for being smart enough to know this is the exception, not the rule in journalism.

And the world keeps on turning.

Postscript: The Star used this column on June 2, 2003. For some obscure reason as I write this postscript, I recall as a kid seeing a sticker on the rear bumper of a car which I think, by changing a few words, would be appropriate for all journalists to remember. It said, "JUST WATCH THE CAR BEHIND THE ONE AHEAD OF YOU!" And I will.

Let's Hear it for the Loners

Don't you think it's about time somebody stepped up to the plate to say a few words on behalf of "The loner?" Okay, so I'm nominated. I accept this great responsibility with humility but determination.

We've had a lot of problems with loners in recent years. There was Ted Kaczynski, the Unibomber, who liked to kill and maim his victims individually and Tim McVeigh, who preferred the mass murder route.

Our latest loner to get his 15 minutes of fame is Charles Bishop, a Florida kid who should never have been given the car keys and certainly not access to an expensive airplane. I started flying lessons at about the same age out of cow pasture in Oklahoma, and the plane's owner would never have let me play around with his old World War II surplus trainer.

Young Charles, who flew a Cessna 172 into a bank building in Florida a few days ago, is taking a real beating in the media for being "a loner." The guest on Bill Maher's "Politically Incorrect" show Thursday night were especially vicious. Conclusion: Loners are not just loners, they are all evil people.

I'm not defending Charles Bishop. But let's not let this business of loners all being killers or pariahs get out of control.

Remember Charles Lindbergh? Arguably one of America's greatest heroes of all time, Lindy was a world-class loner known as "The Lone Eagle." He was, incidentally, one of the few Americans ever to be a recipient of the Congressional Medal of Honor without having served a single day in combat.

How about Albert Einstein? Do you really think he and Mrs. Einstein hosted intimate little dinner parties in Princeton three or four times a week? I don't think so.

Google the bios on these folks and see what you think: Joe DiMaggio, Lou Gehrig, President Truman, Jonas Salk, Dr. Seuss and Amelia Earhart.

Then there is Muhammad Ali. A big entourage always surrounds world champion prizefighters. Right?

I never saw Ali in his prime so I can't say what company he kept. I did meet him years ago when the two senators from Kentucky hosted a reception at the U.S. Capitol, when Ali came and left alone.

Not long afterwards I was in Chicago's O'Hare Airport when I saw Ali come off a plane. The night before he had been featured at a live entertainment gala on television from Los Angeles. In O'Hare he walked alone carrying his hang-up bag and a briefcase cheerily greeting anyone who recognized him.

Finally, how about Wolfgang Amadeus Mozart. My favorite story about him indicates he indeed was a loner.

A young man about eight or nine came up to Mozart at a social event, and asked the great maestro to tell him how he could write a major symphony.

Mozart told the youngster if he would keep studying and working at his music, perhaps some day he could compose something important.

"But," responded the kid, "you were writing great symphonies when you were my age!"

"That's true," said Mozart. "The difference is, I wasn't asking someone to tell me how to do it."

Postscript: I think of all the columns I've written for the Arizona Daily Star, used on Jan. 20, 2001, this one received more response than any of the others. Some readers did not as usual send an email to the Star wanting my email address, they tracked me down in the phone book or the Internet and called to say it was time someone stood up for the loners.

Yes, 'Young People' Was Rejected

When I submitted this column to the Arizona Daily Star it was rejected with the reasoning I had not made my case.

I didn't argue, but I thought of a story told me many years ago by an official of what now is called the Agency for International Development—our foreign aid program.

He said two priests who had been working among the teeming masses in Calcutta, India, long before the world had heard of Mother Teresa, were talking about the hopelessness of their jobs.

"You know," said one priest, "the answer to the problem here is birth control."

"But, "said his companion, "you know the Holy Father's position on birth control."

"Yes I do know the Holy Father's position on birth control," responded the other priest. "But the problem is the Holy Father has never been to Calcutta."

For the Arizonans who read this and might be offended, I can tell them that high school teachers and college-level faculty with years of experience in the Grand Canyon State shared my view in this column.

Perhaps some day the editor will be teaching at the University of Arizona, Pima Community College or elsewhere in the state. If so, I believe it will not take him long to admit I had a point after all.

Yes, Young People, There Is an Arizona

As our youths head back to school in the next few weeks, I think of one of my favorite songs. It's Jamie O'Neal's "There Is No Arizona," a plaintiff tune about lost love on her "Shiver" CD from Mercury Records.

The boyfriend of the young woman in the song has gone off to Arizona, and has vowed to send for her so they can start a new life "under the never-ending blue sky." Except he never does.

The girl left behind concludes, "There is no Arizona, no Painted Desert, no Sedona, and if there was a Grand Canyon she could fill it up with the lies he told her."

Thus, our state and some of its popular tourist sites become metaphors for promises made and promises not kept.

What adult has not been down Jamie's road, paved with disappointment and despair? Even children experience disillusionment with a friend who steals a favorite toy or a sibling who rats out a brother or sister to the parents.

It seems to me Jamie O'Neal should come to Arizona and write another song about lost hope. It could go something like this:

"There is no New York City
"No chance to ever make it big
"Now, isn't that a pity?"

Sadly, what I have found with many young people here is that no one really wants to make it big in New York City—or anywhere else.

During the two years I taught journalism as an adjunct at Pima Community College, I was greatly disappointed by so many students with so much potential who seemed collectively to have no more ambition than to make it through the day.

When inviting guest speakers for my classes, I implored them to devote as much time to inspiration as to sharing information.

There have been occasional rays of hope, such as a 37-year-old man who quit construction work to study at Pima so he could be a sportswriter. Finding him capable of realizing this ambition, I suggested he leave school and go for it.

He now has two years of solid experience writing sports for a good Texas newspaper. We met for lunch recently while he was on vacation in Tucson, and he seemed happy as a clam. Another of my older Pima students has moved on to the Tucson Citizen staff.

In my moments of remorse about the lack of ambition among Arizona's youth, it's instructional to remember the educational odyssey with my daughter and two sons.

The three are graduates of a high school recently ranked as No.15 among all public high schools in America. Each did just enough work to pass and get a diploma.

My daughter, after graduation, took a few courses at a community college and then left for an extended stay as a tourist in France.

The next graduate, my oldest son, went to work as an aide to a Congressman immediately after leaving high school. Then he thumbed around this country for a time before spending years in France and Spain.

My youngest son entered a good university with a scholarship the fall after graduation, but dropped out after a year.

In time my daughter came home and worked her way through the University of Maryland, graduating with honors. She now has an MBA.

While in his 30s, my oldest son finally returned to the U.S. and, on his own, earned a degree from the University of North Carolina.

My youngest son went back to school, found a job and was graduated from Virginia Commonwealth University in Richmond, Va. After graduation he spent a year trying to make an album of songs with a friend. Earlier this year, he was named Congressional correspondent for the New York Daily News.

At some point in my Pima classes I usually suggested the students look down at their feet. "Are they stuck in the sand?" I asked.

In time I hope the wonderful pool of talent among Arizona's youth will not succumb to the hopelessness of Jamie O'Neal's forlorn lass, but with the wings of Mercury on their feet and hope in their hearts will find it truly is possible to fly.

'Tucson Goodness' Column

Most likely it was my truly eternal optimism that gave me the idea for this column. It was used in the Arizona Daily Star on Dec. 23, 2003.

In the five years since I moved from my probably too long stay in Washington, DC to the Tucson area, some of the crimes committed here have been about as horrendous as evil doing can be. And I say that after living all those years with countless godawful crimes in Washington, DC.

After I moved to Arizona, on an ABC-TV "Nightline" program Tucson was called "the marijuana capital of the world." And Tucson civic leaders did not organize a massive public relations effort to refute this accusation.

Here's the one of all those crimes that is the most memorable.

A Tucson couple took in a friend who apparently otherwise would have been homeless. After finding this man was using library computers to view child pornography, police raided the home and found a child porn tape. The tape was confiscated but the tape's owner was not held for trial.

A short time later the man went to a restaurant on the north side of Tucson around noon. Armed, his objective was to hold those eating in the restaurant hostage until the police gave him back his child porn tape.

An unmarried couple came to the restaurant for lunch. The male stayed outside to smoke while the female, pregnant, went inside to use the restroom. When she emerged, the hostage taker apparently thought she was a threat and killed her.

But as the Tucson and other area media fed us these horror stories, I saw a community where the vast majority had a large and giving heart.

Among the goodness I listed in the column was Jim Click who, because he has for years done his own auto sales commercials, is without doubt the best known person in Southern Arizona. There are scores who could not even tell you the name of the governor here, but everyone knows Jim Click.

Cut from my version submitted to the Star was that Jim Click and I grew up in Western Oklahoma in communities (Rocky and Altus) about 40 miles apart, and while I greatly admire his public service he doesn't seem like someone I would want to go out with for a beer.

So even before my column appeared in the paper, some other good things began to happen.

A reporter at the Star, tipped off by the editor of the editorial page, called to verify that the White Elephant (a Goodwill kind of store) had just given more than a million dollars to schools and charities in Green Valley where it operates and I live. He wrote a piece used the next day.

On Christmas Eve, the major story on the front page of the Star was about Jim Click stepping in to make up a charity's shortfall of the normal amount it collected over the holidays.

On Christmas Day, the Star's lead editorial was one praising Click for his outstanding work in supporting worthy community causes.

It isn't the nature of the news business to bring the good news. But one Christmas in Tucson it did. I do not know if my "Tucson Goodness" column was responsible for what followed. I like to think so.

See Lots of Evil,
Too Little Good

Too point of this guest column is about good, not evil, and I hope you'll stay with me to the end.

Having lived in Washington, DC, and two of its suburbs for a long time before moving to the Tucson area three years ago, I am accustomed to hearing news about violent crime.

Back in the days of Mayor Marion Barry, Washington once was known as the murder capital of the world.

During the pre-sniper era in Washington we had one major drug kingpin who somewhat changed the rules of violence, having no reservations about killing women and children close to anyone who crossed him.

He eventually was convicted and sent off to prison. It was one of those rare cases where a felon was able to take his mother with him while doing hard time.

That was because she was convicted as his partner in crime.

Closer to home, there was a brief period when the Washington area became somewhat terrorized by one or more criminal groups known as "the silver gangs."

The thief or thieves would go to a home, such as that of one of my neighbors in McLean, VA, take a pillowcase and in minutes sweep though the residence taking the silver and expensive jewelry.

Then 22 years ago on Dec. 5, 1980, a one-man silver gangster named Bernard Welch was surprised by one of my friends and his wife when they came home to feed their dogs after dining out and before going to a movie.

The friend was Dr. Michael Halberstam, a Washington cardiologist and brother of David Halberstam, the Pulitzer Prize-winning journalist.

Michael confronted Welch in the living room and was shot before the thief ran for his Mercedes parked on a nearby street. Halberstam got in his car with his wife to drive to the emergency room at the closest hospital.

Sadly, Michael died just before he reached the emergency room. But en route he spotted Welch on the street near where he had parked his Mercedes and ran over him. Welch now is serving a prison term of 140 years.

As violent as were the crimes of the drug dealer and Bernard Welch, in my view they do not compare to some committed since I came to the Tucson area.

Two recent incidents come to mind.

One is the young man who allegedly killed a mother and her two little children just to get the wheels on her car.

The second is the man who killed a pregnant woman in a local restaurant, while ostensibly taking hostages to bargain with police for the return of a kiddy porn tape they had confiscated.

But while these and other crimes are being committed in our community, a world of overwhelming goodness is being performed here every day.

Last month, for instance, my sister, a friend and I decided we would volunteer to cook, serve or clean up at the places where the homeless and others in need were being served Thanksgiving Dinner.

I called every place I could think of and volunteered our services. Guess what. Not only were all well staffed, they told me their volunteer waiting lists were so long there was not a chance our help would be needed.

Now at this holiday season good deeds abound. KGUN-9 is leading an effort to stuff city buses with toys for kids who otherwise would not be getting gifts from Santa.

The station on my pickup radio, 94.9, has its diaper drive going again this year as well as asking listeners to donate blood at the American Red Cross.

The White Elephant nonprofit store in Green Valley just gave a million dollars to deserving local organizations.

And that is just the tip of the iceberg with the Salvation Army and other charitable groups hard at work as usual on their missions of good will.

Finally, I think this community should pay a special tribute to the good deeds of one of the best-known citizens between Phoenix and the Mexican border—auto dealer Jim Click.

Jim Click and I grew up about 40 miles apart in what is known as the "shortgrass country" of Western Oklahoma.

Even so, I'm not sure he is someone I would invite to have a beer. But since moving to this area I find his altruistic footprints everywhere I go.

A year or so ago I attended a kickoff event at La Paloma where he and his wife gave away a new, limited edition Ford Thunderbird for a raffle. Any local nonprofit organization could sell tickets at $100 a pop and keep 100 percent of what they sold. My memory is it raised something like a million dollars.

And while teaching at Pima Community College, I learned Click supports numerous programs there including the new Pima Storm football team. Moreover, he sent one of his top executives to aid Coach Jeff Scurran working with the kickers.

Last year, ABC's "Nightline" program called Tucson the marijuana capital of the world.

Maybe it is.

But maybe Ted Koppel, the "Nightline" anchor, should come out and take another look at the Old Pueblo.

He also might find Tucson is a strong contender for the capital of good will, competing with many other communities across America where sharing too often goes unnoticed and the recounting of evil usually prevails.

Gracias

I'm ending this collection with a letter I wrote to Melena, my youngest granddaughter.

Melena was born July 3, 2003, in the Washington, DC area. Her parents are my youngest son, James, and his wife, Jessica. Obviously, since I live in the Tucson area I don't get a lot of face time with the kid.

But as Christmas, 2004, was approaching, James and Jessica told me Melena had virtually no interest in her rather large collection of toys. She loved books instead—to look through and to have her parents read the stories.

So, as her Christmas gift I bought a large scrapbook at Wal-Mart and spent two weeks fulltime making Melena a book of her very own. In it I included family photos and, of course, images of two of my neighbors out here on the Sonoran Desert— Wile E. Coyote and the Roadrunner.

As I finished Melena's book I thought I would put on the last page a letter to her. It's all about being grateful.

When I look back on my life the people who have helped me are countless. My family, teachers, friends, military leaders during my service days, university professors, bosses and my associates at various places as I moved through my career and on and on.

Probably in most cases I just thoughtlessly took what they gave and never said "Thanks." But I see the same attitude almost every day one way or the other, so in my ingratitude there is lots of company.

Many of those who have helped are no longer living. However, one Christmas Eve not so long ago I did remember someone I wanted to thank. And that's what my letter to Melena is all about. And for all those who have helped me who are still around, gracias, gracias, gracias.

Letter To Melena

Dear Melena,

Fifty-three years ago on Christmas Day, 1951, I was serving with the Marines thousands of miles from home in the Korean War.

Fortunately, just before the holidays my unit was sent from the front line to a safe area in the rear. Instead of living in a cold, dark hole on the top of a mountain only yards from enemy troops, we could sleep on a cot in a tent with a stove and eat three hot meals a day.

Christmas Day was overcast and bitter cold. But there was a bright spot because the word was passed that a troupe of USO entertainers with major Hollywood stars would be there to put on a show for us. The Marine engineers had built a makeshift theatre with logs, canvas sides and a small stage. The show's stars turned out to be Paul Douglas and Jan Sterling, his beautiful blonde wife.

When Ms. Sterling was introduced she came on the stage dressed in a short-sleeved angora sweater and ballerina skirt.

The first thing she did was pull up the skirt on her right leg to adjust her hose on the garter belt.

We had not seen a female in months, and the Marines went crazy. Then she very slowly and casually did the same thing with her left leg. Today I have no memory of anything else about the show.

Late last Christmas Eve I was alone, and began to think about that USO show and the stars who had given up their posh homes in Hollywood to be there with us on Christmas.

I knew Paul Douglas had died years ago, but I decided to try to find Jan Sterling to thank her for standing on the stage in the miserable cold that day to raise her skirt and the morale of mostly young men at war.

In a relatively brief time using the Internet, I found Ms. Sterling was a resident of a nursing home in the Los Angeles area. I dialed the facility's number and explained to a nurse who answered why I was calling. He said he would see if Ms. Sterling could take the call, but returned to report she already was asleep.

The nurse suggested I write a note and fax it to him, promising he would give it to her on Christmas Day. And I did.

So far as I know, she read my note of gratitude for being in Korea to entertain us on Christmas, only one of several shows they performed for the troops that day. Last March Jan Sterling, 83, passed away after a series of strokes.

The point of this little Christmas story, dear Melena, is that as you go through life you should never forget to express your gratitude to those who take the time or make sacrifices to brighten your days. Your parents, teachers, friends and so many others who will serve in this role.

Because, as I learned last Christmas Eve, even after 52 years it is never too late to say thanks to someone who traveled a long way to help hundreds of homesick Marines have a merry, merry Christmas.

With Much Love,
Granddad